The Gospel In Dostoyevsky

Illustrations by Fritz Eichenberg

The Gospel in Dostoyevsky
Selections From His Works

a word from
J. I. Packer
foreword by
Malcolm Muggeridge

introduction by
Ernest Gordon

PLOUGH PUBLISHING HOUSE

Farmington PA 15437, USA
Robertsbridge, East Sussex TN32 5DR, U.K.

Basically a reproduction in English of Volume 20 of the Source Books of Christian Witnesses throughout the Centuries, edited by Eberhard Arnold and published by the Eberhard Arnold-Verlag, Sannerz and Leipzig. Volume 20: "Das Evangelium in Dostojewski," 1927. The notes introducing each selection are translations of Karl Nötzel or are by the editors.

The translations of Constance Garnett were revised and edited for this edition. Nötzel's translations into the German were often very helpful. The excerpt from *The Adolescent (A Raw Youth)* was translated by Andrew R. MacAndrew and reprinted by permission of Doubleday & Co. The illustrations are reprinted by courtesy of Fritz Eichenberg, Associated American Artists, The Heritage Club, and The Limited Editions Club. The cover and frontispiece "Portrait of Dostoyevsky" is from a Fritz Eichenberg wood engraving 4" x 2¾".

The editors wish to express gratitude for the essential help and advice received from Ernest Gordon, Philip Yancey, and C. J. G. Turner.

Library of Congress Cataloging-in-Publication Data

Dostoyevsky, Fyodor, 1821-1881.
    The gospel in Dostoyevsky.
    Summary: A collection of excerpts from Dostoyevsky's writings, demonstrating his spiritual thoughts and grouped under such headings as "Man's Rebellion Against God" and "Life in God."
    1. Dostoyevsky, Fyodor, 1821-1881 — Translations, English. 2. Dostoyevsky, Fyodor, 1821-1881 — Religion. [1. Dostoyevsky, Fyodor, 1821-1881 — Religion] I. Eichenberg, Fritz, 1901- , ill. II. Title.
PG3326.A15 1988   891.73'3   86-30578

ISBN 0-87486-187-X (pbk. : alk. paper)

Contents

A Word from J. I. Packer

Dostoyevsky is to me both the greatest novelist, as such, and the greatest Christian storyteller, in particular, of all time. His plots and characters pinpoint the sublimity, perversity, meanness, and misery of fallen human adulthood in an archetypal way matched only by Aeschylus and Shakespeare, while his dramatic vision of God's amazing grace and of the agonies, Christ's and ours, that accompany salvation, has a range and depth that only Dante and Bunyan come anywhere near. Dostoyevsky's immediate frame of reference is Eastern Orthodoxy and the cultural turmoil of nineteenth-century Russia, but his constant theme is the nightmare quality of unredeemed existence and the heartbreaking glory of the incarnation, whereby all human hurts came to find their place in the living and dying of Christ the risen Redeemer. In the passages selected here, a supersensitive giant of the imagination projects a uniquely poignant vision of the plight of man and the power of God. If it makes you weep and worship, you will be the better for it. If it does not, that will show that you have not yet seen what you are looking at, and you will be wise to read the book again.

Regent College, Vancouver
14 March 1987

Foreword

Like so many of my generation, I first read Dostoyevsky's novel, *Crime and Punishment*, when I was very young. I read it like a thriller, with mounting excitement. Later, when I came to read Dostoyevsky's other works, especially his great masterpiece, *The Brothers Karamazov*, I realized that he was not just a writer with a superlative gift for storytelling, but that he had a special insight into what life is about, into man's relationship with his Creator, making him a prophetic voice looking into and illumining the future. I came to see that the essential theme of all his writing is Good and Evil, the two points round which the drama of our mortal existence is enacted.

Dostoyevsky was a God-possessed man if ever there was one, as is clear in everything he wrote and in every character he created. All his life he was questing for God, and found Him only at the end of his days after passing through what he called "the hell-fire of doubt." Freedom to choose between Good and Evil he saw as the very essence of earthly existence. "Accept suffering and be redeemed by it" — this was Dostoyevsky's message to a world hurrying frenziedly in the opposite direction; seeking to abolish suffering and find happiness. Since Dostoyevsky's time, the world has known much

1

trouble and found little happiness, and so may be the better disposed to heed his words.

Dostoyevsky, who normally stayed as far away as possible from museums and art galleries, paid a special visit to the Museum of Art in Basel to see a painting, "Christ Taken Down from the Cross," by Hans Holbein the Younger. He had heard about this picture, and what he had heard had greatly impressed him. His wife Anna in her Diary described Dostoyevsky's reaction to seeing the original:

> The painting overwhelmed Fyodor Mikhailovich, and he stopped in front of it as if stricken . . . On his agitated face was the sort of frightened expression I had often noted during the first moments of an epileptic seizure. I quietly took my husband's arm, led him to another room and made him sit down on a bench, expecting him to have a seizure any minute. Fortunately, it didn't come. Little by little Fyodor Mikhailovich calmed down, and when we were leaving he insisted on going to take another look at the painting that had made such an impression on him.

Anna's own reaction was one of revulsion. She writes of the painting that, contrary to tradition, Christ is depicted "with an emaciated body, the bones and ribs showing, the hands and feet pierced by wounds, swollen and very blue, as in a corpse that is beginning to rot. The face is agonized, and the eyes are half open, but unseeing and expressionless. The nose, mouth, and chin have turned blue."

The reason that Anna was so horrified was that Holbein's picture shows the body of Christ in a state of decomposition. On the other hand, as far as Dostoyevsky was concerned, the picture's fascination was precisely that it *did* show Christ's body decomposing. If His body was not subject to decay like other bodies, then the sacrifice on the Cross was quite meaningless; Christ had to be a man like other men in order to die for men. In other words, at the Incarnation, God did truly become a Man.

Dostoyevsky was a truly prophetic figure, plunging

down frenziedly into his kingdom of hell on earth and arriving at Golgotha. He had a tremendous insight into the future and foresaw the world we have today. He also proclaimed the coming of a universal brotherhood brought about, not by socialism and revolution, but by the full and perfect realization of Christian enlightenment.

In the serener circumstances of his last years, Dostoyevsky's essential love of life and joy in all God's creation found a surer expression than ever before. "Beauty", he makes Dmitri Karamazov say, "is not only a terrible thing, it is also a mysterious thing. There God and the Devil strive for mastery, and the battleground is the heart of men."

I continue to marvel at the chance — if chance it was — whereby the works of one of the greatest Christian writers of modern times should have continued to circulate in the world's first avowedly atheistic state — Dostoyevsky's devastatingly penetrating exposition of sin and suffering and redemption. Supposing one were asked to name a book calculated to give an unbeliever today a clear notion of what Christianity is about, could one hope to do much better than *The Brothers Karamazov*?

Malcolm Muggeridge

Introduction

This book of excerpts from the writing of Dostoyevsky begins, very rightly, with "The Legend of the Grand Inquisitor," from *The Brothers Karamazov*. This is the high point of the stories he incorporates into his novels and essays. They are similar to the parables told by Jesus. They provide the reader with a practical illustration of a universal truth that can be described in no other way. "The Legend of the Grand Inquisitor" is a superb parable of human existence. It raises the great, or cursed, questions so characteristic of Dostoyevsky's passion for the *living* Gospel. Only in the light of the Gospel is the complexity of human existence made understandable, purposeful, and hopeful. Without it there is no meaning to the daily round of human life.

One might expect the Legend to be narrated by a believer. It is not. It is a prose poem composed by Ivan (p. 57), the Karamazov brother who is the rationalist and the man of "the Euclidean mind." He, like the believer, is passionately involved in the Gospel but in terms of its rejection, because it does not conform to his logic or his demand for "justice." He cannot understand why the world is arranged as it is. The only logical thing left for him to do is to return his ticket to existence. But to whom is he to return it? "And so I hasten to give back my entrance ticket, and if I am an honest man, I am

5

bound to give it back as soon as possible. And that I am doing. It's not God that I don't accept, Alyosha, only I most respectfully return him the ticket." Thus the idea of God is essential even for someone who is trying passionately to deny Him.

Alyosha, the believing brother, understands this tormented position and classifies it as rebellion; the rebellion of the disbeliever, who must have "justice." If he cannot have it, then he has no recourse but to destroy himself. In analyzing his brother's position Alyosha is describing man after the fall, man in rebellion against God, man seeking to be as God. Thus sin is not passive but active; not simply a failure to obey God's command, but a deliberate refusal to obey; indeed, an act of defiance.

Ivan, in telling "The Legend of the Grand Inquisitor," is thus telling his own story. He rebels against God's ordering of creation and denies the effectiveness of Christ's redemption. His Euclidean mind rejects the reality of God, man, and nature because it does not measure up to his formula of justice. Although he agonizes over the suffering of innocent children, he does so nevertheless, not from his love of them, but rather from his idea of its injustice. He confesses, "I never could understand how one can love one's neighbors. It's just one's neighbors, to my mind, that one can't love, though one might love people at a distance." "One can love one's neighbors in the abstract" (pp. 43, 44). Such is the position of the Grand Inquisitor.

For love of humanity he has assumed the burden of its freedom, a freedom too great for the people to bear. In assuming this burden he has chosen the way of the three temptations, which Jesus rejected for the sake of freedom. Thus he tells Jesus, "At last we have completed that work in Thy name . . . Today people are more persuaded than ever that they have perfect freedom, yet they have brought their freedom to us and laid it humbly at our feet" (pp. 24, 25).

The freedom to which the Grand Inquisitor refers is the freedom of illusion. At best it is an idea and no more than that. Thus he believes himself to be justified in giving the masses bread in exchange for its soul. The mystery of his ideology replaces the divine mystery. By means of it the people assume that the bondage enforced by "the sword of Caesar" is indeed the freedom they seek.

The tragic irony of Ivan's situation is thus reflected in the image of the Grand Inquisitor. Both of them understand the mystery of the Gospel as the mystery of divine/human freedom, yet they cannot accept it. They are in bondage. In rejecting the deliverance offered to them in the God–man they have chosen to be the man–God; the man who rules the Tower of Babel, or any tyranny in any time and in any place. It is on this note that the Legend ends. Jesus whom the Grand Inquisitor has condemned, kisses "his bloodless, aged lips." "The kiss glows in his heart, but the old man adheres to his idea." For the sake of his idea he condemns Jesus who is the Word become flesh. The passion of his Euclidean thinking leaves him with no alternative.

Dostoyevsky raises the question about the Gospel: What is it? The answer is that it is the good news of our deliverance. St. Paul's great affirmation in Galatians 5:1 is the triumphant note of freedom achieved for us in and by Christ, "For freedom Christ set us free." This is not just an idea invented by scholars. It is the costly action of God in His freedom. This freedom has awful consequences. We have the freedom to defy the living God who has created us. What we term the Fall is an act of freedom. It is a negative freedom, however; it is that of rebellion. This is our condition without God — rebels who are driven by pride to assume what they imagine to be the power of God over others. We claim the freedom to sin, but we are unwilling to assume its consequences. We turn to Satan for justification, as the Grand Inquisitor (or Ivan) did. He is their invention as the justifier of their rebellion. These are the Grand Inquisitor's words: "The wise and dread spirit, the spirit of self-destruction and nonexistence, the great spirit talked with Thee [Jesus] in the wilderness." For both him and Ivan the miracle is not our Lord's rejection of the three temptations, but their own invention and preservation of them. They are "the whole future history of the world and of humanity" (p. 25). They represent the choice of human pride, the original sin.

Although humankind has chosen to rebel against God, God has not rebelled against it and all its members. His love will not let them go. Makar presents this truth, "I'd be frightened to meet a truly godless man . . . I've never really met a man like that. What I have met were restless men, for that's what they should really be called . . . They come from all classes, even the lowest . . . but it's all restlessness" (p. 227). This restlessness describes the situation of all who were called to be pilgrims on the way to the Eternal City but have lost their way because they have lost sight of their destination. They have, therefore, given away their inheritance and lost their destiny, like the Prodigal Son. God, however, is there! He has made us for Himself!

Dostoyevsky seems to be indicating that man without God is nothing. The background for his writing is that of nineteenth century secularism. The "Enlightenment" had surpassed the Reformation to affirm as truth the idea of a godless cosmos, in which the state is supreme and its subjects have lost the dignity of the divine image. Erich Fromm was correct in stating that the intellectuals got rid of God in the eighteenth century and of man in the nineteenth. Dostoyevsky reminds us, however, that God and man cannot be destroyed by this idea. Perhaps two of the darkest rebels are the old father Karamazov, who represents the collective sin of Russia, and Stavrogin in *The Possessed*, who is the second generation rebel and revolutionary. Like Lenin and his successors, Stavrogin had come to the position of assuming that without God all things such as terrorism and murder — are permissible. The Elder Zossima describes such a condition as hell; he reflects upon the question, "What is hell?" and answers it by replying that it is "the suffering of being unable to love." Such is the awful consequence of the freedom granted to us to negate God, and with Him our origin and destiny.

Creative freedom, on the other hand, is an act of Grace. The Gospel bears witness to the only One who was and is truly free. Like the pious people of the peasantry, Dostoyevsky saw the humiliation of God in Jesus, as it is described by St. Paul in Philippians 2:5–11, as the essence of the Gospel. This humiliation as the essence of the Gospel is, however, a phase of the divine exaltation in which we are included. In this respect the teaching of Irenaeus in the second century A.D. had a great deal of influence upon the spiritual life of the Russian Orthodox Church. His teaching is more timely than ever: namely, God became man that man might become one with God.

In *Crime and Punishment* Dostoyevsky tells the story of Raskolnikov, who believes himself to be liberated from the old morality of Christian culture to the extent that he is free to murder a woman whom he presumes to be a useless member of society. His crime appears to be without purpose and without passion. He is one of those who prides himself upon his inability to love. Yet it is by the love of Sonia, a Russian version of Mary Magdalene, that he is claimed by Grace. He sees in her "a sort of insatiable compassion" which leads him to his first act of repentance (p. 123). While still trying to believe in his freedom from God he turns to her, bends down, drops to the ground, and kisses her foot (p. 128). This irrational act adds to his confusion to the extent that he tries to dismiss her as a "religious maniac." Nevertheless, he asks her to read the miracle of the raising of Lazarus. This she does. In doing so she reads it in such a way that her reading of it is her great confession: "Yea, Lord: I believe that thou art the Christ, the son of God Which should come into the world." (p. 134). By her faith the power of Grace that brought Lazarus from the corruption of the grave is repeated in the experience of Raskolnikov. He has the assurance that by this Grace he will be forgiven at the Last Judgment. He is thus liberated from the bondage of sin, guilt, and fear.

As Sonia, the humiliated woman, is the agent of Raskolnikov's redemption, so the humiliated people of Russia will be the agent of its deliverance from the consequences of the sin of the nineteenth century intellectuals (p. 241). This is a prophecy that may well be in the process of being fulfilled at this moment. "But God will save Russia as He has saved her many times. Salvation will come from the people, from their faith and their weakness." It is those who share in the fellowship of suffering that share in the liberating action of the living God. The eyes of their faith are opened by Grace so that they behold the mystery of God revealed in Christ's agony on the Cross. They understand, as the intellectuals cannot, that their salvation is beyond rational knowledge. It is of faith, for faith is our response to God's revelation in Christ.

At this point it may be well to think about Dostoyevsky's free characters. Three in particular are:

1) The underground man — or the equivalent of the ant who exists under the floorboards — is the man who dares to be free no matter how irrational such a claim may be. Despite the rational structuring of society and the attempted abolition of human freedom, he refuses to be a stop in the organ

that can be pulled and pressed at the command of some superorganist. He is free to be absurd and to defy the system.

2) Prince Myshkin of *The Idiot* is the aristocrat who disregards the position granted to him by birth and wealth in order to take his place among the people in his freedom to be a fool in the eyes of his peers for Christ's sake. His identity is with the humiliated Christ, and as such he is called upon to engage in His acts of deliverance. In his love for Nastasya Filippovna he is moved to bring — or at least to make the attempt to bring — Christ's salvation to her, mad though she may be. In doing so he is reflecting the image of Christ — thus incurring the wrath of his critics who abuse and despise him and yet inwardly love him, even as the repentant rebel on the Cross turned to Jesus beseeching deliverance. In describing the witness of the Prince, Dostoyevsky seems to be drawing upon the image of the suffering Messiah of Isaiah 52:13–53:12, which in turn is similar to the great kenotic passage in Philippians 2; Prince Myshkin thus is free to suffer. This is the cross he has accepted.

3) Alyosha is the pilgrim, and disciple, who learns that by repentance we participate in the benefits of Christ's deliverance and are thus set free to love and to be responsible. Like Raskolnikov he is captured by Grace. It is not his doing nor even of his seeking. Salvation is a happening beyond the control of church or state. It is an ecstasy of response to the wind of God that blows where it wills.

The miracle of Grace in Alyosha's life is related to Christ's first miracle at the wedding feast at Cana of Galilee. By the narration of this miracle Alyosha becomes aware that Christ visits people in their gladness to intensify their joy. Again, it is the humiliated who possess the gladness to respond ecstatically to the joy of Christ.

It is the Elder Zossima, who in reflecting the Grace of Jesus, leads Alyosha into His presence. By him he was called to participate in the joy of the celebration. Thus, in his dream, he perceives that the dead Elder Zossima is alive in the power of the resurrection. It is to this life eternal that he is invited as the Elder Zossima takes him by the hand to raise him from his knees. As he rises he hears the staretz say, "We are drinking the new wine, the wine of new, great gladness."

Suddenly the mystery is revealed. His soul is filled to overflowing with rapture. In his ecstasy he throws himself down on the earth to kiss it and water it with his tears. By this unprecedented act "He had fallen on the earth a weak boy, but he rose up a resolute champion . . . 'Someone visited my soul in that hour'" (p.215). How similar this is to the humiliation and exaltation of Raskolnikov.

Alyosha not only waters the earth with his tears and loves the stars, he also assumes the responsibility of "all men's sins." By such an act of love he fulfills the purpose of his freedom and participates in God's continuing work of redemption. It is only by such love that he learns to "perceive the divine mystery in things" (p. 246). This exhortation by Zossima is a moving poem of agape. In such love we may understand better the beatitude of the meek inheriting the earth.

Alyosha is the Christian who, in his freedom, responds to the living Gospel. In responding he freely accepts responsibility for the sins and salvation of his fellow sinners. He loves *in* the love of Christ. By such love the condemnation of the ultimate judgment is overcome, and the mystery of the revelation is understood. Behind such a position we may note the good news of John 3:16: God loved, God gave His Son, God gives eternal life, God sets us free from the bondage of sin. Along with it is the testimony of St. John in the fourth chapter of his first letter: "God is love . . . There is no room for fear in love; perfect love banishes fear . . . We love because He loved us first." Dostoyevsky's love of the Gospel is thus clearly evident in his writings, and Alyosha reflects his own pilgrimage to the City of God, the Kingdom which is not of this world.

Dostoyevsky's hosanna of faith was hammered out on the anvil of doubt. Doubt does not imply ignorance, nor denial of the Gospel, but rather the testing of the truth of the Gospel. He tells in his *Diary of a Writer* that he was brought up in a pious Russian family. He received instruction in the Gospel "almost from the cradle." Such an upbringing was unusual among the Russian intellectuals of that time. Their interest was not in the Church and the tradition it represented but in the apparently new and exciting philosophies of the Enlightenment. The theories of rationalism, romanticism, positivism, agnosticism, humanism, nihilism, anarchism, and communism were standard fare at the dinner tables of the aristocratic intellectuals. It is sometimes affirmed that the tragedy of Russia is that it never enjoyed the civilizing influence of the Renaissance. I do not think this is true. From the time of Peter the Great on the intellectual climate of Russia was influenced by the ideas spawned in the post–Renaissance period of the West. Those of the 19th century expressed the rejection of Christianity and its moral principles, which had contributed to the development of Western democracy. Such was the intellectual atmosphere that involved Dostoyevsky in the struggle of faith.

His writings reveal that he remembered a great deal of his early Christian education. The book of Job made a lasting impression upon him. It is the story of the righteous man who suffered and through his suffering came to participate in a personal dialogue with the living God. What had once been hearsay was transcended into fact by meeting God face-to-face. In seeing God, Job repented in humiliation through which his former life of superficial righteousness was discarded for the righteousness of the right relationship granted to him by the action of God. Reference to this spiritual experience is made by Staretz Zossima in his account of his fascination with Job at the age of eight.

Along with his instruction in the Gospel went instruction in the stories of the saints. The one that made a deep impression on him was the account of a fourteenth-century Russian saint by the name of Sergey. This saint lived as a hermit in the forest, sustaining himself daily by a piece of bread. One day he encountered a large bear at the entrance of his hut. Instead of running away, the saint befriended the bear and shared his meager rations with him. Thereafter, the bear visited him daily. Dostoyevsky refers to this story in *The Brothers Karamazov*. Its influence is obvious in Staretz Zossima's great poem of love: "Love all God's creation . . . Love the animals, love the plants, love everything."

Another influence was that of the monks in their monasteries (pp. 237, ff). Dostoyevsky regarded them as expressing the purest form of spiritual life. They turned away from the lusts of the flesh and worldly power to be with God, to identify with the poor and the outcasts just as Jesus had done, and to serve them in love. Thus the portrait Dostoyevsky gives us of his ideal Christian is that of Zossima, who like himself had once been a slave of pride. In his pride and anger and for no reason, he had mercilessly beaten his batman (servant) in the army. By repentance he participated in the new life of the Spirit and in utter humility sought the forgiveness of the peasant he had wronged.

The publication of his *Poor Folk* in 1846 may mark the time of his change from being a conventional Christian to becoming a radical socialist and atheist. Belinsky befriended him and hailed his book as a work of great literary art. The radical intellectuals of this period regarded Belinsky as their hero. In following his leadership Dostoyevsky took the way that led to his arrest and the death sentence in 1849. At the moment of execution he was reprieved. We may imagine what a traumatic experience that was. It marks the change from the intellectual dilettante playing with ideas like a Greek hero–God to his involvement with sinners as a sinner. He gives us a description of this terrifying moment in *The Idiot* when he describes the scene of the mass of people come to watch the execution and the loneliness of the victim. As spectators they watch the priest holding the cross for the victim to kiss "with his blue lips" (p. 153).

After this reprieve he served four years of hard labor and then five years of exile in Siberia. Those were years of utter humiliation. His very moving *The House of the Dead*, which was written from his diary, tells the story of his suffering and his depression. It was "a time of living burial." It was also the time of his crucifixion and resurrection. On his way to prison a woman thrust a New Testament into his hand. This provided him with the means of entering into and dwelling in the passion and exaltation of Jesus. Suffering had become a way of the cross for him even after his return from Siberian exile. His lot was one of sickness, poverty, debts, and overwork. The fruits of his suffering, however, are his literary achievements. Because of his debts he was forced to become an exile, yet once again. In this exile he wrote *The Idiot* and *The Possessed.*

As well as being a description of his degradation, *The House of the Dead* is a metaphor of human existence similar to the one used earlier by Pascal: namely, we are all cast into the death cell, and we experience daily our own death in the death of the other. This may be regarded as the basis of Christian existentialism. Descartes' famous dictum, *Cogito, ergo sum* (I think, therefore I am), presumes that reason precedes existence. This is the fallacious premise which closed the Fabian intellect of Ivan Karamazov to the primacy of existence. But sin is not a failure of conditioning or an unwholesome idea. It is the major fact of the human condition. It was this fact that turned Dostoyevsky from Belinsky and his nihilistic revolutionary theories, to Christ and His Gospel. *The Possessed* (or *The Devils*) is an illustration of the descent from utopian socialism to the blind black pit of demonic rebellion. It is also a prophecy of Russia's future, in which it would surrender to the Temptations of "wonder" bread and power and give its soul to the Grand Inquisitor.

The awful nature of evil as our rebellion against God, which Dostoyevsky portrayed so vividly, has troubled many of his critics. He has been judged as a pathologically disturbed person unduly fascinated by the despair of depression. Such a criticism is in essence a reflection of the Euclidean mind. The romantic vision of a utopia governed by the ideologically enlightened "philosopher kings" is one that ignores our present existence. Such utopias are seldom more than the projections of the present place and time idealized in order to conform to our judgments. In other words, they are constructed from what is at hand, including the injustices we wish to correct. One example of this is Freud's analysis of Dostoyevsky in which he accused him of denigrating acceptable morality by plunging his characters into the pit of evil and then exalting them, as in the case of Raskolnikov, to the heights of moral excellency. Another example is that of a critic who described Dostoyevsky as "The Rasputin of literature." In the manner of Ivan, such critics can allow no place for the acceptance of the mystery of Grace.

Admittedly his works could be described as psychopathological but only by those who are ignorant of the Gospel he came to love so well. The Good News is that God in Christ has entered into our condition to the extent of dying for us on the Cross. He is with us, that is, at the moment of our ultimate failure, to transform it into the beauty of eternal life. By faith, we enjoy the wonder of Christ's presence. As at the Wedding Feast at Cana, His presence is an occasion of great joy.

The present revival of religion in the Soviet Union owes much to Dostoyevsky and his early admirers. He has made an enormous contribution to the Christian thinkers who have been, and are, leaders in this spiritual reformation. Perhaps the best and most revealing testimony to his witness is that made by Nicholas A. Berdyaev in his admirable book *Dostoyevsky*. He writes, "He stirred and lifted up my soul more than any other writer or philosopher has done, and for me people are always divided into 'dostoyevskyites' and those to whom his spirit is foreign . . . 'The Legend of the Grand Inquisitor,' in particular, made such an impression on my young mind that when I turned to Jesus Christ for the first time, I saw him under the appearance that He bears in the Legend."

Ernest Gordon
Author of *Miracle on the River Kwai*

FAITH IN GOD — MAN'S VENTURE

The Legend of the Grand Inquisitor

This "prose poem" from The Brothers Karamazov *is probably the climax of Dostoyevsky's religious confessions. It is recited by Ivan Karamazov, who refuses to recognize God although he admits God's existence.*

"He came softly, unobserved, and yet, strange to say, everyone recognized Him. The people are irresistibly drawn to Him, they surround Him, they flock about Him, follow Him. He moves silently in their midst with a gentle smile of infinite compassion. The sun of love burns in His heart; light and power shine from His eyes; and their radiance, shed on the people, stirs their hearts with responsive love. He holds out His hands to them and blesses them and a healing virtue comes from contact with Him, even with His garments. An old man in the crowd, blind from childhood, cries out, 'O Lord, heal me and I shall see Thee!' and as it were, scales fall from his eyes and the blind man sees Him. The people weep and kiss the earth under His feet. Children throw flowers before Him, sing, and cry hosannah. 'It is He — it is He!' all repeat. 'It must be He, it can be no one but He!' He stops at the steps of the Seville cathedral at the moment when the weeping mourners are bringing in a little open white coffin. In it lies a child of seven, the only daughter of a prominent citizen. The dead child lies hidden in flowers. 'He will raise your child,' the crowd shouts to the weeping mother. The priest, coming to meet the coffin, looks perplexed and

21

frowns, but the mother of the dead child throws herself at His feet with a wail. 'If it is You, raise my child!' she cries, holding out her hands to Him. The procession halts, the coffin is laid on the steps at His feet. He looks with compassion, and His lips once more softly pronounce, 'Talitha cumi!' and the maiden arises. The little girl sits up in the coffin and looks round, smiling with wide-open wondering eyes, holding white roses they had put in her hand.

"There are cries, sobs, confusion among the people, and at that moment the cardinal himself, the Grand Inquisitor, passes by the cathedral. He is an old man, almost ninety, tall and erect, with a withered face and sunken eyes, in which there is still a gleam of light. He is not dressed in his gorgeous cardinal's robes, as he was the day before, when he was burning the enemies of the Roman Church — at this moment he is wearing his coarse, old monk's cassock. At a distance behind him come his gloomy assistants and slaves and the 'holy guard.' He stops at the sight of the crowd and watches it from a distance. He sees everything; he sees them set the coffin down at His feet, sees the child rise up, and his face darkens. He knits his thick grey brows and his eyes gleam with a sinister fire. He holds out his finger and bids the guards take Him. And such is his power, so completely are the people cowed into submission and trembling obedience to him, that the crowd immediately make way for the guards, and in the midst of deathlike silence they lay hands on Him and lead Him away. The crowd, like one man, instantly bows down to the earth before the old inquisitor. He blesses the people in silence and passes on. The guards lead their prisoner to the close, gloomy vaulted prison in the ancient palace of the Holy Inquisition and shut Him in it. The day passes and is followed by the dark, burning, breathless night of Seville. The air is fragrant with laurel and lemon. In the pitch darkness the iron door of the prison is suddenly opened and the Grand Inquisitor himself comes in with a light in his hand. He is alone; the door is closed at once behind him. He stands in the doorway and for a minute or two gazes into His face. At last he goes up slowly, sets the light on the table and speaks.

"'Is it You? You?' but receiving no answer, he adds at once, 'Don't answer, be silent. What can You say, indeed? I know too well what You would say. And You have no right to add anything to what You have said of old. Why then, are You come to hinder us? For You have come to hinder us, and You know that. But You know what will be tomorrow? I know not who You are and care not to know whether it is You or only a semblance of Him, but tomorrow I shall condemn You and burn You at the stake as the worst of heretics. And the very people who have today kissed Your feet, tomorrow at the faintest sign from me will rush to heap up the embers of Your fire. Know You that? Yes, maybe You know it,' he added with thoughtful penetration, never for a moment taking his eyes off the Prisoner."

"I don't quite understand, Ivan. What does it mean?" Alyosha, who had been listening in silence, said with a smile. "Is it simply a wild fantasy, or a mistake on the part of the old man — some impossible confusion?"

"Take it as the last," said Ivan, laughing, "if you are so corrupted by modern realism and can't stand anything fantastic. If you like it to be a case of mistaken identity, let it be so. It is true," he went on, laughing, "the old man was ninety, and he might well be crazy over his set idea. He might have been struck by the appearance of the Prisoner. It might, in fact, be simply his ravings, the delusion of an old man of ninety, over-excited by the auto-da-fé of a hundred heretics the day before. But does it matter to us after all whether it was a mistake of identity or a wild fantasy? All that matters is that the old man should speak out, should speak openly of what he has thought in silence for ninety years.''

"And the Prisoner too is silent? Does He look at him and not say a word?''

"That's inevitable in any case,'' Ivan laughed again. "The old man has told Him He hasn't the right to add anything to what He has said of old. One may say it is the most fundamental feature of Roman Catholicism, in my opinion at least. 'All has been given by You to the Pope,' he says, 'and all, therefore, is still in the Pope's hands, and there is no need for You to come now at all. You must not meddle for the time, at least.' That's how they speak and write too — the Jesuits, at any rate. I have read it myself in the works of their theologians.

" 'Have You the right to reveal to us one of the mysteries of that world You have come from?' my old man asks Him, and answers the question for Him. 'No, You have not; so You may not add to what has been said of old, and may not take from men the freedom which You exalted when You were on earth. Whatever You might reveal anew will encroach on men's freedom of faith; for it will be manifest as a miracle, and the freedom of their faith was dearer to You than anything in those days fifteen hundred years ago. Did You not often say then, "I will make you free"? But now You have seen these "free" men,' the old man adds suddenly, with a pensive smile. 'Yes, we've paid dearly for it,' he goes on, looking sternly at Him, 'but at last we have completed that work in Your name. For fifteen centuries we have been wrestling with Your freedom, but now it is ended and over for good. Do You not believe that it's over for good? You look meekly at me and do not deign even to be wroth with me. But let me tell You that now, today, people are more persuaded than ever that they have perfect freedom, yet they have brought their freedom to us and laid it humbly at our feet. But that has been our doing. Was this what You did? Was this Your freedom? . . .

" 'The wise and dread spirit, the spirit of self-destruction and non-existence' the old man goes on, 'the great spirit talked with You in the wilderness, and we are told in the books that he "tempted" You. Is that so? And could anything truer be said than what he revealed to You in three questions and what You rejected, and what in the books are called "the temptations"? And yet if there has ever been on earth a real and stupendous miracle, it took place on that day, on the day of the three temptations. The statement of those three questions was itself the miracle. If it were possible to imagine simply for the sake of argument that those three questions of the dread spirit had perished utterly from the books and that we had to restore them and to invent them anew and to do so had gathered together all the wise men of the earth — rulers, chief priests, learned men, philosophers, poets — and had set them the task to invent three questions such as would not only fit the occasion but express in three words, three human phrases, the whole future history of the world and of humanity — do You believe that all the wisdom of the earth brought together could have invented anything in depth and force equal to the three questions which were actually put to You then by the wise and mighty spirit in the wilderness? From those questions alone, from the miracle of their statement, we can see that we have to do here not with the fleeting human intelligence but with the absolute and eternal. For in those three questions the whole subsequent history of mankind is foretold, as it were, gathered together into one whole and uniting in them all the unsolved historical contradictions of human nature. At the time it could not be so clear, since the future was unknown; but now that fifteen hundred years have passed, we see that everything in those three questions was so rightly divined and foretold and so truly fulfilled that nothing can be added to them or taken from them.

"'Judge Yourself who was right — You or he who questioned You then. Remember the first question; its meaning, in other words, was this: "You would go into the world, and are going with empty hands, with some promise of freedom that men in their simplicity and their natural unruliness cannot even understand, that they fear and dread — for nothing has ever been more unbearable for a man and a human society than freedom. But see You these stones in this parched and barren wilderness? Turn them into bread, and mankind will run after You like a flock of sheep, grateful and obedient, though for ever trembling, lest You withdraw Your hand and deny them Your bread." But You would not deprive man of freedom and rejected the offer, thinking, "What is that freedom worth if obedience is bought with bread?" You replied that man lives not by bread alone. But do You know that for the sake of that earthly bread the spirit of the earth will rise up against You and will strive with You and overcome You, and all will follow him, crying, "Who can compare with this beast? He has given us fire from heaven!" Do You know that the ages will pass, and humanity will proclaim by the lips of their sages that there is no crime, and therefore no sin; there is only hunger? "Feed men, and then ask of them virtue!" That's what they'll write on the banner they will raise against You, with which they will destroy Your temple. Where Your temple stood will rise a new building; the terrible tower of Babel will be built again, and though, like the one of old, it will not be finished, yet You might have prevented that new tower and have cut short the sufferings of men by a thousand years; for they will come back to us after a thousand years of agony with their tower. They will seek us again, hidden underground in the catacombs, for we shall be again persecuted and tortured. They will find us and cry to us, "Feed us, for those who have promised us fire from heaven haven't given it!" And then we shall finish building their tower, for he who feeds them finishes the building. And we alone shall feed them in Your name, declaring falsely that it is in Your name. Oh, never, never can they feed themselves without us! No science will give them bread so long as they remain free. In the end they will lay their freedom at our feet and say to us, "Make us your slaves, but feed us." They themselves will understand at last that freedom and bread enough for all are inconceivable together, for never, never will they be able to share fairly between them! They will be convinced, too, that they can never be free, for they are weak, vicious, worthless, and rebellious.

"'You promised them the bread of Heaven, but I repeat again, can it compare with earthly bread in the eyes of the weak, ever sinful and ever ignoble race of man? And if for the sake of the bread of Heaven thousands and tens of thousands will follow You, what is to become of the millions and tens of thousands of millions of creatures who will not have the strength to forego the earthly bread for the sake of the heavenly? Or do You care only for the tens of thousands of the great and strong while the millions, numerous as the sands of the sea, who are weak but love You must exist only for the sake of the great and strong? No, we care for the weak too. They are sinful and rebellious, but in the end they too will become obedient. They will marvel at us and look on us as gods because we are ready to endure freedom and rule over them — so awful will freedom seem to them.

"'But we shall tell them that we are Your servants and rule them in Your name. We shall deceive them again, for we will not let You come near us again. That deception will be our suffering, for we shall be forced to lie. This is the significance of the first question in the wilderness, and this is what You rejected for the sake of that freedom which You exalted above everything. Yet in this question lies hidden the great secret of this world. Choosing "bread," You would have satisfied the universal and everlasting craving of humanity — to find someone to worship. So long as man remains free he strives for nothing so incessantly and so painfully as to find someone to worship. But man seeks to worship what is established beyond dispute, so that all men would agree at once to worship it. For these pitiful creatures are concerned not only to find what one or the other can worship but to find something that all would believe in and worship; what is essential is that all may be *together* in it. This craving for *community* of worship is the chief misery of every man individually and of all humanity from the beginning of time. For the sake of common worship they've slain each other with the sword. They have set up gods and challenged one another, "Put away your gods and come and worship ours, or we will kill you and your gods!" And so it will be to the end of the world, even when gods disappear from the earth; they will fall down before idols just the same. You knew, You could not help knowing, this fundamental secret of human nature, but You rejected the one infallible banner which was offered You to make all men bow down to You alone — the banner of earthly bread; and You rejected it for the sake of freedom and the bread of Heaven. Behold what You did further. And all again in the name of freedom! I tell You that man is tormented by no greater anxiety than to find someone quickly to whom he can hand over that gift of freedom with which the ill-fated creature is born. But only the one who can appease their conscience can take over their freedom. In bread there was offered You an invincible banner; give bread, and man will worship You, for nothing is more certain than bread. But if someone else gains possession of his conscience — oh! then he will cast away Your bread and follow after the one who has ensnared his conscience. In that You were right. For the secret of man's being is not only to live but to have something to live for. Without a clear conception of the object of life, man would not consent to go on living and would rather destroy himself than remain on earth, though he had bread in abundance. That is true. But what happened? Instead of taking men's freedom from them, You made it greater than ever! Did You forget that man prefers peace and even death to freedom of choice in the knowledge of good and evil? Nothing is more seductive for man than his freedom of conscience, but nothing is a greater cause of suffering. And behold, instead of giving a firm foundation for setting the conscience of man at rest forever, You chose all that is exceptional, vague, and enigmatic; You chose what was utterly beyond the strength of men, acting as though You did not love them at all — You who came to give Your life for them! Instead of taking possession of men's freedom, You increased it, and burdened the spiritual kingdom of mankind with its sufferings forever. You desired man's free love so that he should follow You freely, enticed and taken captive by You. In place of the rigid, ancient law, man must hereafter with free heart decide for himself what is good and what is evil, having only Your image before him as his guide. But did You not know he would at last reject even Your image and Your truth if he is weighed down with the fearful burden of free choice? They will cry aloud at last that the truth is not in You, for they could not have been left in greater confusion and suffering than You have caused, laying upon them so many cares and unanswerable problems.

"'So that, in truth, You Yourself laid the foundation for the destruction of Your kingdom, and no one is more to blame for it. Yet what was offered You? There are three-powers, three powers alone, able to conquer and hold captive forever the conscience of these impotent rebels for their own happiness — those forces are miracle, mystery, and authority. You have rejected all three and have set the example for doing so. When the wise and dread spirit set You on the pinnacle of the temple and said to You, "If You would know whether You are the Son of God, then cast Yourself down, for it is written: the angels shall hold him up lest he fall and bruise himself, and You shall know then whether You are the Son of God and shall prove then how great is Your faith in Your Father." But You refused and would not cast Yourself down. Oh! of course, You did proudly and well, like God; but the weak, unruly race of men, are they gods? Oh, You knew then that in taking one step, in making one movement to cast Yourself down, You would be tempting God and have lost all Your faith in Him, and would have been dashed to pieces against that earth which You came to save. And the wise spirit that tempted You would have rejoiced.

"'But I ask again, are there many like You? And could You believe for one moment that men too could face such a temptation? Is the nature of men such that they can reject miracles and at the great moments of their life, the moments of their deepest, most agonizing spiritual difficulties, cling only to the free verdict of the heart? Oh, You knew that Your deed would be recorded in books, would be handed down to remote times and the utmost ends of the earth, and You hoped that man, following You, would cling to God and not ask for a miracle. But You did not know that when man rejects miracles, he rejects God too; for man seeks not so much God as the miraculous. And as man cannot bear to be without the miraculous, he will create new miracles of his own for himself and will worship deeds of sorcery and witchcraft, though he might be a hundred times over a rebel, heretic, and infidel. You did not come down from the Cross when they shouted to You, mocking and reviling You, "Come down from the cross and we will believe that You are He." You did not come down, for again You would not enslave man by a miracle and craved faith given freely, not based on miracle. You craved love freely given and not the base raptures of the slave before the might that has overawed him forever. But You thought too highly of men therein, for they are slaves, of course, though rebellious by nature. Look round and judge: fifteen centuries have passed; look upon them. Whom have you raised up to Yourself? I swear, man is weaker and baser by nature than You have believed him! Can he, can he do what You did? By showing him so much respect, You did, as it were, cease to feel for him for You asked far too much from him — You who have loved him more than Yourself! Respecting him less, You would have asked less of him. That would have been more like love, for his burden would have been lighter. He is weak and vile. What though he is everywhere now rebelling against our power, and proud of his rebellion? It is the pride of a child and a schoolboy. They are little children rioting and barring out the teacher at school.

" 'But their childish delight will end; it will cost them dear. They will cast down temples and drench the earth with blood. But they will see at last, the foolish children, that though they are rebels, they are impotent rebels, unable to keep up their own rebellion. Bathed in their foolish tears, they will recognize at last that He who created them rebels must have meant to mock at them. They will say this in despair, and their utterance will be a blasphemy that will make them more unhappy still, for man's nature cannot bear blasphemy, and in the end always avenges it on itself. And so unrest, confusion, and unhappiness — that is the present lot of man after You bore so much for their freedom!

" 'Your great prophet tells in vision and in image that he saw all those who took part in the first resurrection and that there were of each tribe twelve thousand. But if there were so many of them, they must have been gods, not men. They had borne Your cross, they had endured scores of years in the barren, hungry wilderness, living upon locusts and roots — and You can indeed point with pride at those children of freedom, of love freely given, of free and splendid sacrifice for Your name. But remember that they were only some thousands — and what of the rest? And how are the other weak ones to blame because they could not endure what the strong have endured? How is the weak soul to blame that it is unable to receive such terrible gifts? Can You have simply come to the elect and for the elect? But if so, it is a mystery and we cannot understand it. And if it is a mystery, we too have a right to preach a mystery and to teach them that it's not the free judgment of their hearts, not love that matters, but a mystery that they must follow blindly, even against their conscience. So we have done.

"'We have corrected Your work and have founded it upon *miracle, mystery* and *authority*. And men rejoiced that they were again led like sheep and that the terrible gift that had brought them such suffering was at last lifted from their hearts. Were we right teaching them this? Speak! Did we not love mankind when so meekly acknowledging their feebleness, lovingly lightening their burden, and permitting their weak nature even sin with our sanction?

"'Why have You come now to hinder us? And why do You look silently and searchingly at me with Your mild eyes? Be angry. I don't want Your love, for I love You not. And what use is it for me to hide anything from You? Don't I know to Whom I am speaking? All that I can say is known to You already. And is it for me to conceal from You our mystery? Perhaps it is Your will to hear it from my lips. Listen, then. We are not working with You but with *him* — that is our mystery. It's long — eight centuries — since we have been on *his* side and not on Yours. Just eight centuries ago, we took from him what You rejected with scorn, that last gift he offered You, showing You all the kingdoms of the earth. We took from him Rome and the sword of Caesar, and proclaimed ourselves sole rulers of the earth, though hitherto we have not been able to complete our work. But whose fault is that?

" 'Oh, the work is only beginning, but it has begun. It has long to await completion and the earth has yet much to suffer, but we shall triumph and shall be Caesars, and then we shall plan the universal happiness of man. But You might even then have taken the sword of Caesar. Why did You reject that last gift? Had You accepted that last counsel of the mighty spirit, You would have accomplished all that man seeks on earth — that is, some one to worship, some one to keep his conscience, and some means of uniting all in one unanimous and harmonious ant-heap; for the craving for universal unity is the third and last anguish of men. Mankind as a whole has always striven to organize a universal state. There have been many great nations with great histories, but the more highly they were developed the more unhappy they were, for they felt more acutely than other people the craving for worldwide union. The great conquerors, Timurs and Genghis Khans, whirled like hurricanes over the face of the earth striving to subdue its people, and they too were but the unconscious expression of the same craving for universal unity. Had You taken the world and Caesar's purple, You would have founded the universal state and have given universal peace. For who can rule men if not he who holds their conscience and their bread in his hands? We have taken the sword of Caesar, and in taking it we of course have rejected You and followed *him*. Oh, ages are yet to come of the confusion of free thought, of their science and cannibalism. For having begun to build their tower of Babel without us, they will end with cannibalism. But then the beast will crawl to us and lick our feet and spatter them with tears of blood. And we shall sit upon the beast and raise the cup, and on it will be written, "Mystery." But then, and only then, the reign of peace and happiness will come for men.

"'You are proud of Your elect, but You have only the elect, while we give rest to all. And besides, how many of those elect, those mighty ones who could become elect, have grown weary waiting for You and have transferred and will transfer the powers of their spirit and the warmth of their heart to the other camp and end by raising their *free* banner against You. You Yourself lifted up that banner. But with us all will be happy and will rebel no more nor destroy one another as under Your freedom.

"'Oh, we shall persuade them that they will only become free when they renounce their freedom to us and submit to us. And shall we be right or shall we be lying? They will be convinced that we are right, for they will remember the horrors of slavery and confusion to which Your freedom brought them. Freedom, free thought, and science will lead them into such straits and will bring them face to face with such marvels and insoluble mysteries that some of them, the fierce and rebellious, will destroy themselves; others, rebellious but weak, will destroy one another; while the rest, weak and unhappy, will crawl fawning to our feet and whine to us: "Yes, you were right, you alone possess His mystery, and we come back to you — save us from ourselves!"

"'Receiving bread from us, they will see clearly that we take from them the bread made by their hands to give it to them without any miracle. They will see that we do not change the stones to bread, but in truth they will be more thankful for taking it from our hands than for the bread itself! For they will remember only too well that in the old days, without our help, even the bread they made turned to stones in their hands, while since they have come back to us, the very stones have turned to bread in their hands. Too, too well they know the value of complete submission! And until men know that, they will be unhappy. Who is most to blame for their not knowing it? Speak! Who scattered the flock and sent it astray on unknown paths? but the flock will come together again, will submit once more, and then it will be for good. Then we shall give them the quiet, humble happiness of weak creatures such as they are by nature. Oh, we shall persuade them at last not to be proud, for You lifted them up and thereby taught them to be proud. We shall show them that they are weak, that they are only pitiful children, but that childlike happiness is the sweetest of all. They will become timid and will look to us and huddle close to us in fear, as chicks to the hen. They will marvel at us and will be awe-stricken before us and will be proud at our being so powerful and clever that we have been able to subdue such a turbulent flock of thousands of millions. They will tremble impotently before our wrath, their minds will grow fearful, they will be quick to shed tears like women and children, but they will be just as ready at a sign from us to pass to laughter and rejoicing, to happy mirth and childish song. Yes, we shall set them to work, but in their leisure hours we shall make their life like a child's game, with children's songs and innocent dance.

" 'Oh, we shall allow them even sin — they are weak and helpless — and they will love us like children because we allow them to sin. We shall tell them that every sin will be expiated if it is done with our permission, that we allow them to sin because we love them, and that the punishment for these sins we take upon ourselves. And we shall take it upon ourselves, and they will adore us as their saviors who have taken on themselves their sins before God. And they will have no secrets from us. We shall allow or forbid them to live with their wives and mistresses, to have or not to have children — according to whether they have been obedient or disobedient — and they will submit to us gladly and cheerfully. They will bring to us all the most painful secrets of their conscience — all — and we shall have an answer for everything. And they will be glad to believe our answer, for it will save them from the great anxiety and terrible agony they endure at present in making a free decision for themselves. And all will be happy, all the millions of creatures except the hundred thousand who rule over them. For only we, we who guard the mystery, shall be unhappy. There will be thousands of millions of happy babes and a hundred thousand sufferers who have taken upon themselves the curse of the knowledge of good and evil. Peacefully they will die, peacefully they will expire in Your name, and beyond the grave they will find nothing but death. But we shall keep the secret, and for their happiness we shall allure them with the reward of heaven and eternity. Though if there were anything in the other world, it certainly would not be for such as they.

" 'It is prophesied that You will come again in victory, You will come with Your chosen, the proud and strong, but we will say that they have only saved themselves, whereas we have saved all. We are told that the harlot who sits upon the beast and holds in her hands the *mystery* shall be put to shame, that the weak will rise up again and will rend her royal purple and will strip naked her loathsome body. But then I will stand up and point out to You the thousand millions of happy children who have known no sin. And we who have taken their sins upon us for their happiness will stand up before You and say: "Judge us if You can and dare." Know that I fear You not. Know that I too have been in the wilderness, I too have lived on roots and locusts, I too prized the freedom with which You have blessed men, and I too was striving to stand among Your elect, among the strong and powerful, thirsting "to make up the number." But I awakened and would not serve madness. I turned back and joined the ranks of those *who have corrected Your work.* I left the proud and went back to the humble for the happiness of the humble. What I say to You will come to pass, and our dominion will be built up. I repeat, tomorrow You shall see that obedient flock who at a sign from me will hasten to heap up the hot cinders about the pile on which I shall burn You for coming to hinder us. For if anyone has ever deserved our fires, it is You. Tomorrow I shall burn You. I have spoken.'

"When the Inquisitor ceased speaking, he waited some time for his Prisoner to answer him; His silence weighed down upon him. He saw that the Prisoner had listened intently all the time, looking gently in his face and evidently not wishing to reply. The old man longed for Him to say something, however bitter and terrible. But He suddenly approached the old man in silence and softly kissed him on his bloodless, aged lips. That was all his answer. The old man shuddered. His lips moved. He went to the door, opened it, and said to Him: 'Go, and come no more — come not at all, never, never!' And he let Him out into the dark alleys of the town. The Prisoner went away."

"And the old man?"

"The kiss glows in his heart, but the old man adheres to his idea."

MAN'S REBELLION
AGAINST GOD

Rebellion

In The Brothers Karamazov *"Rebellion" immediately precedes "The Legend of the Grand Inquisitor." Like this legend it is directed by Ivan to Alyosha Karamazov, his younger brother, who is a novice living in a monastery outside the city.*

"I must make you one confession," Ivan began. "I could never understand how one can love one's neighbors. It's just one's neighbors, to my mind, that one can't love, though one might love people at a distance. I once read somewhere of John the Merciful, a saint, that when a hungry, frozen beggar came to him, he took him into his bed, held him in his arms, and began breathing into his mouth, which was putrid and loathsome from some awful disease. I am convinced that he did that in self-laceration, in a self-laceration of falsity, for the sake of the charity imposed by duty, as a penance laid on him. A man must be hidden for anyone to love him, for as soon as he shows his face, love is gone."

"Father Zossima has talked of that more than once," observed Alyosha. "He, too, said that the face of a man often hinders many people not practised in love from loving him. But yet there's a great deal of love in mankind, almost Christ-like love. I know that myself, Ivan."

"Well, I know nothing of it so far, and can't understand it, and the innumerable mass of mankind are with me there. The question is whether that's due to men's bad qualities or

43

whether it's inherent in their nature. To my thinking, Christ-like love for men is a miracle impossible on earth. He was God. But we are not gods. Suppose I, for instance, suffer intensely. No one else can ever know how much I suffer, because he is another and not I. And what's more, a man is rarely ready to admit another's suffering (as if it were a distinction). Why won't he admit it, do you think? — because I smell bad, because I have a stupid face, because I once trod on his foot. Besides there is suffering and suffering; degrading, humiliating suffering such as humbles me — hunger, for instance — my benefactor will perhaps allow me; but when you come to higher suffering — for an idea, for instance — he will very rarely admit that, perhaps because my face strikes him as not at all what he fancies a man should have who suffers for an idea. And so he deprives me instantly of his favor, not at all from badness of heart. Beggars, especially genteel beggars, ought never to show themselves but ask for charity through the newspapers. One can love one's neighbors in the abstract or even at a distance, but at close quarters it's almost impossible. If it were as on the stage, in the ballet, where if beggars come in, they wear silken rags and tattered lace and beg for alms dancing gracefully, then one might like looking at them. But even then we should not love them.

"But enough of that. I simply wanted to show you my point of view. I meant to speak of the suffering of mankind generally, but we had better confine ourselves to the sufferings of children. That reduces the scope of my argument to a tenth of what it would be. Still we'd better keep to the children, though it does weaken my case. For in the first place, children can be loved even at close quarters, even when they are dirty, even when they are ugly (though I fancy children are never ugly). The second reason why I won't speak of grown-up people is that, besides being disgusting and unworthy of love, they have a compensation — they've eaten the apple and know good and evil, and they have become 'like gods.' They go on eating it still. But the children haven't eaten anything, and so far are innocent.

"Are you fond of children, Alyosha? I know you are, and you will understand why I prefer to speak of them. If they too suffer horribly on earth, they must suffer for their fathers' sins, they must be punished for their fathers, who have eaten the apple; but that reasoning is of the other world and is incomprehensible for the heart of man here on earth. The innocent must not suffer for another's sins, and especially such innocents! You may be surprised at me, Alyosha, but I am awfully fond of children, too. And observe — cruel people, the violent, the rapacious, the Karamazovs, are sometimes very fond of children. Children while they are quite little — up to seven, for instance — are so remote from grown-up people; they are different creatures, as it were, of a different species. I knew a criminal in prison who had, in the course of his career as a burglar, murdered whole families, including several children. But when he was in prison, he had a strange affection for them. He spent all his time at his window, watching the children playing in the prison yard. He trained one little boy to come up to his window and made great friends with him . . . You don't know why I am telling you all this, Alyosha? My head aches and I am sad."

"You speak with a strange air," observed Alyosha uneasily, "as though you were not quite yourself."

"By the way, a Bulgarian I met lately in Moscow," Ivan went on, seeming not to hear his brother's words, "told me about the crimes committed by Turks and Circassians in all parts of Bulgaria through fear of a general uprising of the Slavs. They burn villages, murder, outrage women and children, they nail their prisoners by the ears to the fences, leave them so till morning, and in the morning they hang them — all sorts of things you can't even imagine. People talk sometimes of bestial cruelty, but that's a great injustice and insult to the beasts; a beast can never be so cruel as a man, so artistically cruel. The tiger only tears and gnaws, that's all he can do. He would never think of nailing people by the ears, even if he were able to do it. These Turks took a pleasure in torturing children too; cutting the unborn child from the mother's womb, and tossing babies up in the air and catching them on the points of their bayonets before their mother's eyes. Doing it before the mother's eyes was what gave zest to the amusement. Here is another scene that I thought very interesting. Imagine a trembling mother with her baby in her arms, a circle of invading Turks around her. They've planned a diversion; they pet the baby, laugh to make it laugh. They succeed, the baby laughs. At that moment a Turk points a pistol four inches from the baby's face. The baby laughs with glee, holds out its little hands to the pistol, and he pulls the trigger in the baby's face and blows out its brains. Artistic, wasn't it? By the way, Turks are particularly fond of sweet things, they say."

"Brother, what are you driving at?" asked Alyosha.

"I think if the devil doesn't exist but man has invented him, he has created him in his own image and likeness."

Just as he did God, then?" observed Alyosha.

" 'It's wonderful how you can turn words,' as Polonius says in *Hamlet*," laughed Ivan. "You turn my words against me. Well, I am glad. Yours must be a fine God, if man created Him in his own image and likeness. You asked just now what I was driving at. You see, I am fond of collecting certain facts, and would you believe, I even copy anecdotes of a certain sort from newspapers and books, and I've already got a fine collection. The Turks, of course, have gone into it, but they are foreigners. I have specimens from home that are even better than the Turks. You know we prefer beating — rods and scourges — that's our national institution. Nailing ears is unthinkable for us, for we are, after all, Europeans. But the rod and the scourge we have always with us and they cannot be taken from us. Abroad now they scarcely do any beating. Manners are more humane, or laws have been passed, so that they don't dare to flog men now. But they make up for it in another way just as national as ours. And so national that it would be practically impossible among us, though I believe we are being inoculated with it, since the religious movement began in our aristocracy.

"I have a charming pamphlet, translated from the French, describing how quite recently (five years ago) a murderer, Richard, was executed — a young man of twenty-three, I believe — who repented and was converted to the Christian faith at the very scaffold. This Richard was an illegitimate child who was given at the age of six by his parents to some shepherds on the Swiss mountains. They brought him up to work for them. He grew up like a little wild beast among them. The shepherds taught him nothing and scarcely fed or clothed him but sent him out at seven to herd the flock in cold and wet, and no one hesitated or scrupled to treat him so. Quite the contrary, they thought they had every right, for Richard had been given to them as a chattel, and they did not even see the necessity of feeding him. Richard himself describes how in those years, like the Prodigal Son in the Gospel, he longed to eat of the mash given to the pigs, which were fattened for sale. But they wouldn't even give him that and beat him when he stole from the pigs. And that was how he spent all his childhood and his youth until he grew up and was strong enough to go away and be a thief.

"The savage began to earn his living as a day laborer in Geneva. He drank what he earned, he lived like a brute, and finished by killing and robbing an old man. He was caught, tried, and condemned to death. They are not sentimentalists there. And in prison he was immediately surrounded by pastors, members of Christian brotherhoods, philanthropic ladies, and the like. They taught him to read and write in prison, and expounded the Gospel to him. They exhorted him, worked upon him, drummed at him incessantly, till at last he solemnly confessed his crime. He was converted. He wrote to the court himself that he was a monster, but that in the end God had vouchsafed him light and shown grace. All Geneva was in excitement about him — all philanthropic and religious Geneva. All the aristocratic and well-bred society of the town rushed to the prison, kissed Richard and embraced him: 'You are our brother, you have found grace.' And Richard does nothing but weep with emotion, 'Yes, I've found grace! All my youth and childhood I was glad of pigs' food, but now even I have found grace. I am dying in the Lord.' 'Yes, Richard, die in the Lord; you have shed blood and must die. Though it's not your fault that you knew not the Lord, when you coveted the pigs' food and were beaten for stealing it (which was very wrong of you, for stealing is forbidden); but you've shed blood and you must die.' And on the last day, Richard, perfectly limp, did nothing but cry and repeat every minute: 'This is my happiest day. I am going to the Lord.' 'Yes,' cry the pastors and the judges and philanthropic ladies. 'This is the happiest day of your life, for you are going to the Lord!' They all walk or drive to the scaffold in procession behind the prison van. At the scaffold they call to Richard: 'Die, brother, die in the Lord, for even thou hast found grace!' And so, covered with his brothers' kisses, Richard is dragged on to the scaffold and led to the guillotine. And they chopped off his head in brotherly fashion, because he had found grace. Yes, that's characteristic.

"That pamphlet is translated into Russian by some Russian philanthropists high in society and sympathetic to Lutheranism and has been distributed gratis for the enlightenment of the people. The case of Richard is interesting because it's national. Though to us it's absurd to cut off a man's head, because he has become our brother and has found grace, yet we have our own speciality, which is not much better. Our historical pastime is the direct satisfaction of inflicting pain. There are lines in Nekrassov describing how a peasant lashes a horse on the eyes, 'on its meek eyes.' Everyone must have seen that. It's peculiarly Russian. He describes how a feeble little nag founders under too heavy a load and cannot move. The peasant beats it, beats it savagely, beats it at last not knowing what he is doing in the intoxication of cruelty, thrashes it mercilessly over and over again. 'However weak you are, you must pull, if you die for it.' The nag strains, and then he begins lashing the poor defenseless creature on its weeping, 'meek eyes.' The frantic beast tugs and draws the load, trembling all over, gasping for breath, moving sideways, with a sort of unnatural spasmodic action — it's awful in Nekrassov. But that's only a horse, and God has given horses to be beaten. So the Tartars taught us, and they left us the knout as a remembrance.

"But men, too, can be beaten. A well-educated, cultured gentleman and his wife beat their own child with a birch rod, a girl of seven. I have an exact account of it. The papa was glad that the birch was covered with twigs. 'It stings more,' said he, and so he began stinging his daughter. I know for a fact there are people who at every blow are worked up to sensual pleasure, to literal sensuality that increases progressively at every blow they inflict. They beat for a minute, for five minutes, for ten minutes, more often and more savagely. The child screams. At last the child cannot scream, it gasps, 'Daddy! daddy!' By some diabolical unseemly chance the case was brought into court. A counsel is engaged. The Russian people have long called a barrister 'a conscience for hire.' The counsel protests in his client's defense. 'It's such a simple thing,' he says, 'an everyday domestic event. A father corrects his child, and to our shame it is brought into court.' The jury, convinced by him, give a favorable verdict. The public roars with delight that the torturer is acquitted. Ah, pity I wasn't there! I would have proposed to raise a subscription in his honor! . . . Charming pictures.

"But I've still better things about children. I've collected a great, great deal about Russian children, Alyosha. There was a little girl of five who was hated by her father and mother, 'most worthy and respectable people of good education and breeding.' You see, I must repeat again, it is a peculiar characteristic of many people, this love of torturing children, and children only. To all other types of humanity these torturers behave mildly and benevolently, like cultivated and humane Europeans; but they are very fond of tormenting children, that even is their fondness of children in a sense. It's just their defenselessness that tempts the tormentor, just the angelic confidence of the child who has no refuge and no appeal, that sets his vile blood on fire. In every man, of course, a demon lies hidden — the demon of rage, the demon of lustful heat at the screams of the tortured victim, the demon of lawlessness let off the chain, the demon of diseases that follow on vice.

"This poor child of five was subjected to every possible torture by those cultivated parents. They beat her, thrashed her, and kicked her for no reason until her body was one bruise. Then, they went to greater refinements of cruelty — shut her up all night in the cold and frost in a privy, and because she didn't ask to be taken up at night (as though a child of five sleeping its angelic, sound sleep could be trained to wake and ask), they smeared her face and filled her mouth with excrement, and it was her mother, her mother who did this. And that mother could sleep, hearing the poor child's groans! Can you understand why a little creature, who can't even understand what's done to her, should beat her little aching heart with her tiny fists in the dark and the cold, and weep her meek unresentful tears to 'dear kind God' to protect her? Do you understand that, friend and brother, you pious and humble novice? Do you understand why this infamy must be and is permitted? Without it, I am told, man could not have existed on earth, for he could not have known good and evil. Why should he know that diabolical good and evil when it costs so much? Why, the whole world of knowledge is not worth that child's prayer to 'dear, kind God'! I say nothing of the sufferings of grown-up people; they have eaten the apple, damn them, and the devil take them all! But these little ones! I am making you suffer, Alyosha, you are not yourself. I'll leave off if you like."

"Never mind. I want to suffer too," muttered Alyosha.

"One picture, only one more, because it's so curious, so characteristic, and I have only just read it in some collection of Russian antiquities. I've forgotten the name. I must look it up. It was in the darkest days of serfdom at the beginning of the century, and long live the Liberator of the People! There was in those days a general of aristocratic connections, the owner of great estates, one of those men — somewhat exceptional, even then I believe — who, retiring from the service into a life of leisure, are convinced that they've earned absolute power over the lives of their subjects. There were such men then.

"So our general, settled on his property of two thousand souls, lives in pomp, and domineers over his poor neighbors as though they were dependents and buffoons. He has kennels of hundreds of hounds and nearly a hundred dog-boys — all mounted and in uniform. One day a serf boy, a little child of eight, threw a stone in play and hurt the paw of the general's favorite hound. 'Why is my favorite dog lame?' He is told that the boy threw a stone that hurt the dog's paw, 'So you did it.' The general looked the child up and down. 'Take him.' He was taken — taken from his mother and kept shut up all night. Early that morning the general comes out on horseback, with the hounds, his dependents, dog-boys and huntsmen, all mounted around him in full hunting parade. The servants are summoned for their edification, and in front of them all stands the mother of the child.

"The child is brought from the lock-up. It's a gloomy, cold, foggy autumn day, a capital day for hunting. The general orders the child to be undressed; the child is stripped naked. He shivers, numb with terror, not daring to cry . . . 'Make him run,' commands the general. 'Run! run!' shout the dog-boys. The boy runs . . . 'At him!' yells the general, and he sets the whole pack of hounds on the child. The hounds catch him and tear him to pieces before his mother's eyes! . . . I believe the general was afterwards declared incapable of administering his estates. Well — what did he deserve? To be shot? To be shot for the satisfaction of our moral feelings? Speak, Alyosha!"

"To be shot," murmured Alyosha lifting his eyes to Ivan with a pale, twisted smile.

"Bravo!" cried Ivan delighted. "If even you say so . . . You're a pretty monk! So there is a little devil sitting in your heart, Alyosha Karamazov!"

"What I said was absurd, but —"

"That's just the point that 'but'" cried Ivan! "Let me tell you, novice, that the absurd is only too necessary on earth. The world stands on absurdities, and perhaps nothing would have come to pass on it without them. We know what we know!"

"What do you know?"

"I understand nothing," Ivan went on, as though in delirium. "I don't want to understand anything now. I want

to stick to facts. I made up my mind long ago not to understand. If I try to understand anything I shall be false to facts
and I have determined to stick to fact.''

"Why are you trying me?" Alyosha cried, with sudden
distress. "Will you say what you mean at last?"

"Of course, I will; that's what I've been leading up to.
You are dear to me, I don't want to let you go, and I won't
give you up to your Zossima.''

Ivan for a minute was silent, his face became all at once
very sad.

"Listen! I took the case of children only to make my case
clearer. Of the other tears of humanity with which the earth is
soaked from its crust to its center, I will say nothing. I have
narrowed my subject on purpose. I am a bug, and I recognize
in all humility that I cannot understand why the world is
arranged as it is. Men are themselves to blame, I suppose; they
were given paradise, they wanted freedom, and they stole fire
from heaven, though they knew they would become unhappy,
so there is no need to pity them. With my pitiful, earthly
Euclidian understanding, all I know is that there is suffering
and that there are none guilty; that cause follows effect,
simply and directly; that everything flows and finds its level —
but that's only Euclidian nonsense. I know that, and I can't
consent to live by it! What comfort is it to me that there are
none guilty and that cause follows effect simply and directly,
and that I know it — I must have justice, or I will destroy
myself. And not justice in some remote, infinite time and
space, but here on earth so that I could see it myself. I have
believed in it. I want to see it, and if I am dead by then, let me
rise again, for if it all happens without me, it will be too
unfair. Surely I haven't suffered, simply that I, my crimes and
my sufferings, may manure the soil of the future harmony for
somebody else. I want to see with my own eyes the lamb lie
down with the lion and the victim rise up and embrace his

murderer. I want to be there when everyone suddenly understands what it has all been for. All the religions of the world are built on this longing, and I am a believer.

"But then there are the children, and what am I to do about them? That's a question I can't answer. For the hundredth time I repeat, there are numbers of questions, but I've only taken the children, because in their case what I mean is so unanswerably clear. Listen! If all must suffer to pay for the eternal harmony, what have children to do with it — tell me please? It's beyond all comprehension why they should suffer and why they should pay for the harmony. Why should they too furnish material to enrich the soil for the harmony of the future? I understand solidarity in sin among men. I understand solidarity in retribution, too; but there can be no such solidarity with children. And if it is really true that they must share responsibility for all their fathers' crimes, such a truth is not of this world and is beyond my comprehension. Some jester will say, perhaps, that the child would have grown up and have sinned, but you see he didn't grow up, he was torn to pieces by the dogs, at eight years of age.

"Oh, Alyosha, I am not blaspheming! I understand, of course, what an upheaval of the universe it will be, when everything in heaven and earth blends in one hymn of praise and everything that lives and has lived cries aloud: 'Thou art just, O Lord, for Thy ways are revealed.' When the mother embraces the fiend who threw her child to the dogs and all three cry aloud with tears, 'Thou art just, O Lord!' then, of course, the crown of knowledge will be reached and all will be made clear. But what pulls me up here is that I can't accept that harmony. And while I am on earth, I make haste to take my own measures. You see, Alyosha, perhaps it really may happen that if I live to that moment, or rise again to see it, I too may perhaps cry aloud with the rest, looking at the mother embracing the child's torturer, 'Thou art just, O Lord!' But I don't want to cry aloud then. While there is still time, I hasten to protect myself and so I renounce the higher harmony altogether. It's not worth the tears of that one tortured child who beat itself on the breast with its little fist and prayed in its stinking outhouse with its unexpiated tears to 'dear, kind God'! It's not worth it, because those tears are unatoned for. They must be atoned for, or there can be no harmony. But how? How are you going to atone for them? Is it possible? By their being avenged? But what do I care for avenging them? What do I care for a hell for oppressors? What good can hell do, since those children have already been tortured? And what becomes of harmony, if there is hell? I want to forgive. I want to embrace. I don't want more suffering.

"And if the sufferings of children go to swell the sum of sufferings which was necessary to pay for truth, then I protest that the truth is not worth such a price. I don't want the mother to embrace the oppressor who threw her son to the dogs! She dare not forgive him! Let her forgive him for herself if she will, let her forgive the torturer for the immeasurable suffering of her mother's heart. But the sufferings of her tortured child she has no right to forgive; she dare not forgive the torturer, even if the child were to forgive him! And if that is so, if they dare not forgive, what becomes of harmony? Is there in the whole world a being who would have the right to forgive and could forgive? I don't want harmony. From love for humanity I don't want it. I would rather be left with the unavenged suffering. I would rather remain with my unavenged suffering and unsatisfied indignation, *even if I were wrong*. Besides, too high a price is asked for harmony; it's beyond our means to pay so much to enter. And so I hasten to give back my entrance ticket, and if I am an honest man, I am bound to give it back as soon as possible. And that I am doing. It's not God that I don't accept, Alyosha, only I most respectfully return Him the ticket."

"That's rebellion," murmured Alyosha, looking down.

"Rebellion? I am sorry you call it that," said Ivan earnestly. "One can hardly live in rebellion, and I want to live. Tell me yourself, I challenge you — answer. Imagine that you are creating a fabric of human destiny with the object of making men happy in the end, giving them peace and rest at last, but that it was essential and inevitable to torture to death only one tiny creature — that baby beating its breast with its fist, for instance — and to found that edifice on its unavenged tears, would you consent to be the architect on those conditions? Tell me, and tell the truth."

"No, I wouldn't consent," said Alyosha softly.

"And can you admit the idea that men for whom you are building it would agree to accept their happiness on the foundation of the unexpiated blood of a little victim? And accepting it would remain happy for ever?"

"No, I can't admit it. Brother," said Alyosha suddenly, with flashing eyes, "you said just now, is there a being in the whole world who would have the right to forgive and could forgive? But there is a Being and He can forgive everything, all and for all, because He gave His innocent blood for all and everything. You have forgotten Him, and on Him is built the edifice, and it is to Him they cry aloud, 'Thou art just, O Lord, for Thy ways are revealed!'"

"Ah! the One without sin and His blood! No, I have not forgotten Him; on the contrary I've been wondering all the time how it was you did not bring Him in before, for usually all arguments on your side put Him in the foreground. Do you know, Alyosha — don't laugh! I made a poem about a year ago. If you can waste another ten minutes on me, I'll tell it to you."

"You wrote a poem?"

"Oh, no. I didn't write it," laughed Ivan, "and I've never written two lines of poetry in my life. But I made up this poem in prose and I remembered it. I was carried away when I made it up. You will be my first reader — that is, listener. Why should an author forego even one listener?'' smiled Ivan. ''Shall I tell it to you?''

''I am all attention,'' said Alyosha.

''My poem is called 'The Grand Inquisitor'; it's a ridiculous thing, but I want to tell it to you.''

The Devil

This is a delirious dream or nightmare of Ivan Karamazov. It is probably unique in world literature as an attempt to portray how the uncontrolled ego of a conscious atheist expresses itself, an atheist who knows a great deal more about God than most believers. The dream has only an inner connection with the novel as a whole. Ivan is physically ill as well. His illness ("brain fever") was caused by outer circumstances, but its hallucinations come from the deepest emotional content of his subconscious.

Ivan had just had a bad inner shake-up after the onset of his illness. Smerdyakov, the servant and illegitimate son of Ivan's murdered father, had confessed to him that it was he who had murdered the older Karamazov, not Ivan's half-brother Dmitri, who was in prison for the crime. To prove the truth of his confession, Smerdyakov handed over to Ivan the 3000 rubles for the sake of which the murder had been committed. He went on to tell Ivan, that it was actually Ivan himself who had mainly incited him, Smerdyakov, to commit this crime. This he had done not only through his godless talking, his continual denial of God's existence; but even more, Smerdyakov had been firmly convinced after an exchange with Ivan before the murder that in committing it he would be acting completely according to Ivan's wishes. Ivan cannot possibly doubt the sincerity of these confessions. Accordingly, he suddenly sees himself as his father's murderer. To escape despair, he now needs God, whom he was unwilling to recognize before.

58

I am not a doctor, but yet I feel that the moment has come when I must of necessity give the reader some account of the nature of Ivan's illness. Looking ahead, I can say at least one thing: he was at that moment on the very eve of an attack of brain fever. Though long affected by it, his health had offered a stubborn resistance to the fever that in the end gained complete mastery. Though I know nothing of medicine, I venture to suggest that perhaps he really had, by a terrible effort of will, succeeded in delaying the attack for a time, hoping of course to check it completely. He knew that he was unwell, but he loathed the thought of being ill at that fateful time, at the approaching crisis in his life, when he needed to have all his wits about him, to say what he had to say boldly and resolutely, and "to justify himself to himself."

He had, however, consulted the new doctor, who had been brought from Moscow by a fantastic notion of Katerina Ivanovna's to which I have referred already. After listening to him and examining him, the doctor came to the conclusion that he was actually suffering from some disorder of the brain and was not at all surprised by an admission that Ivan had reluctantly made to him. "Hallucinations are quite likely in your condition," the doctor said, "though it would be better to verify them . . . you must take steps at once, without a moment's delay, or things will go badly with you." But Ivan did not follow this judicious advice and did not take to his bed to be nursed. "I am walking about, so I am strong enough; if I drop, it will be different — then anyone may nurse me who likes," he decided, dismissing the subject.

And so he was sitting, almost conscious himself of his delirium, and as I have said already, looking persistently at some object on the sofa against the opposite wall. Someone appeared to be sitting there, though goodness knows how he had come in, for he had not been in the room when Ivan came into it on his return from Smerdyakov. This person or, more accurately speaking, this Russian gentleman of a particular type, no longer young, "had made his fiftieth" as the French say, with rather long, still thick, dark hair, slightly streaked with grey, and a small pointed beard. He was wearing a brownish reefer, rather shabby but evidently made by a good tailor and of a fashion that had been discarded by the smart and well-to-do for the last two years. His linen and his long scarflike necktie were such as are worn by people who aim at being stylish, but on closer inspection his linen was not overclean and his wide scarf was very threadbare. The visitor's check trousers were of excellent cut but were too light in color and too tight for the present fashion. His soft fluffy white hat was out of keeping with the season.

In brief there was every appearance of gentility on straitened means. It looked as though the gentleman belonged to that class of idle landowners who used to flourish in the times of serfdom. He had unmistakably been, at some time, in good and fashionable society, had once had good connections, had indeed possibly preserved them, but after a gay youth, becoming gradually impoverished after the abolition of serfdom, he had sunk into the position of a poor relation of the best class, wandering from one good old friend to another and received by them for his companionable and accommodating disposition and as being, after all, a gentleman who could be asked to sit down with anyone, though of course not in a place of honor. Such gentlemen of accommodating temper and dependent position, who can tell a story, take a hand at cards, and who have a distinct aversion for any duties that may be forced upon them, are usually solitary creatures, either bachelors or widowers. Sometimes they have children, but if so the children are always being brought up at a distance, at some aunt's to whom these gentlemen never allude in good society, seeming ashamed of the relationship. They gradually lose sight of their children altogether, though at intervals they receive a birthday or Christmas letter from them and sometimes even answer it.

The countenance of the unexpected visitor was not so much good-natured as accommodating and ready to assume any amiable expression that occasion might require. He had no watch, but he had a tortoise-shell lorgnette on a black ribbon. On the middle finger of his right hand was a massive gold ring with a cheap opal stone in it.

Ivan was angrily silent and would not begin the conversation. The visitor waited and sat exactly like a poor relation who had come down from his room to keep his host company at tea and was discreetly silent, seeing that his host was frowning and preoccupied. But he was ready for any affable conversation as soon as his host should begin it. All at once his face expressed a sudden solicitude.

"I say," he began to Ivan, "excuse me, I only mention it to remind you. You went to Smerdyakov's to find out about Katerina Ivanovna, but you came away without finding out anything about her; you probably forgot . . ."

"Ah, yes," broke from Ivan and his face grew gloomy with uneasiness. "Yes, I'd forgotten . . . but it doesn't matter now, never mind, till to-morrow," he muttered to himself, "and you," he added, addressing his visitor, "I should have remembered that myself in a minute, for that was just what was tormenting me! Why do you interfere? So that I should believe that you prompted me and that I didn't remember it of myself?"

"Don't believe it then," said the gentleman, smiling amicably, "what's the good of believing against your will? Besides, proofs are no help to believing, especially material proofs. Thomas believed, not because he saw Christ risen, but because he wanted to believe before he saw. Look at the spiritualists, for instance . . . I am very fond of them . . . they imagine that they are serving the cause of religion because the devils show them their horns from the other world. They say that is a material proof, so to speak, of the existence of another world. The other world and material proofs — what next! And if you come to that, does proving there's a devil prove that there's a God? I want to join an idealist society, I'll lead the opposition in it, I'll say I am a realist but not a materialist, he-he!''

"Listen," Ivan suddenly got up from the table. "I seem to be delirious . . . I am delirious, in fact; talk any nonsense you like, I don't care! You won't drive me into a fury, as you did last time. But I feel somehow ashamed . . . I want to pace about the room . . . sometimes I don't see you and don't even hear your voice as I did last time, but I always guess what you are prating, for it is I, *I myself speaking, not you*. Only I don't know whether I was dreaming last time or whether I really saw you. I'll wet a towel and put it on my head and perhaps you'll vanish into air.''

Ivan went into the corner, took a towel, and did as he said, and with a wet towel on his head began walking up and down the room.

"I am so glad you treat me so familiarly," the visitor began.

"Fool," laughed Ivan, "do you suppose I should stand on ceremony with you? I am in good spirits now, though I've a pain in my forehead — and in the top of my head — only please don't talk philosophy, as you did last time. If you can't take yourself off, talk of something amusing. Talk gossip; you are a sponger, you ought to talk gossip. What a nightmare to have! But I am not afraid of you. I'll get the better of you. I won't be taken to a madhouse!''

"How charming, a sponger. Yes, I am in my natural shape. For what am I on earth but a poor relation? By the way, I am listening to you and am rather surprised to find you are actually beginning to take me for something real, not simply your fancy, as you persisted in declaring last time . . ."

"Never for one minute have I taken you for reality," Ivan cried with a sort of fury. "You are a lie, you are my illness, you are a phantom. It's only that I don't know how to destroy you, and I see I must suffer for a time. You are my hallucination. You are the incarnation of myself, but only of one side of me — of my thoughts and feelings, but only the most nasty and stupid of them. From that point of view you might be of interest to me, if only I had time to waste on you . . ."

"Excuse me, excuse me, I'll prove it. You flew out at Alyosha under the lamp-post this evening and shouted to him: 'You learnt it from *him*! How do you know that *he* visits me?' You were thinking of me then. So for one brief moment you did believe that I really exist," the gentleman laughed blandly.

"Yes, that was a moment of weakness . . . but I couldn't believe in you. I don't know whether I was asleep or awake last time. Perhaps I was only dreaming then and didn't really see you at all . . ."

"And why were you so surly with Alyosha just now? He is a dear; I've treated him badly over Father Zossima."

"Don't talk of Alyosha! How dare you, you flunkey!" Ivan laughed again.

"You berate me, but you laugh — that's a good sign. But you are ever so much more polite than you were last time and I know why: that great resolution of yours. . ."

"Don't speak of my resolution," cried Ivan savagely.

"I understand, I understand, so noble, so charming, you are going to defend your brother and sacrifice yourself . . . That is chivalrous."

"Hold your tongue, or I'll kick you!"

"I shan't be altogether sorry, for then my object will be attained. If you kick me, you must believe in my reality, for people don't kick ghosts. Joking aside, it doesn't matter to me, abuse me if you like, though it's better to be a trifle more polite even to me. 'Fool, flunkey!' what words!''

"Berating you, I berate myself," Ivan laughed again, "you are myself, myself, only with a different face. You just say what I am thinking . . . and are incapable of saying anything new!''

"If I am like you in my way of thinking, it's all to my credit," the gentleman declared with delicacy and dignity.

"You choose out only my worst thoughts, and what's more, the stupid ones. You are stupid and vulgar. You are awfully stupid. No, I can't put up with you! What am I to do, what am I to do!'' Ivan said through his clenched teeth.

"My dear friend, above all things I want to behave like a gentleman and to be recognized as such," the visitor began in an increase of deprecating but good-natured pride, typical of a sponging relation. "I am poor, but . . . I won't say very honest, but it's an axiom generally accepted in society that I am a fallen angel. I certainly can't imagine how I can ever have been an angel. If I ever was, it must have been so long ago that there's no harm in forgetting it. Now I only prize the reputation of being a gentlemanly person and live as I can, trying to make myself agreeable. I love men genuinely, I've been greatly slandered! Here when I stay with you from time to time, my life gains a kind of reality and that's what I like most of all. You see, like you, I suffer from the fantastic and so I love the realism of earth. Here, with you, everything is circumscribed, here all is formulated and geometrical, while we have nothing but indeterminate equations! Here I wander about dreaming. I like dreaming. Besides, on earth I become superstitious. Please don't laugh, that's just what I like, to become superstitious. I adopt all your habits here: I've grown fond of going to the public baths — would you believe it? And I go and steam myself with merchants and priests. What I dream of is becoming incarnate once for all and irrevocably in the form of some merchant's wife weighing 250 pounds and believing all she believes. My ideal is to go to church and offer a candle in simple-hearted faith, upon my word it is. Then there would be an end to my sufferings. I like being doctored too; in the spring there was an outbreak of smallpox and I went and was vaccinated in a foundling hospital — if only you knew how I enjoyed myself that day. I subscribed ten roubles to the cause of the Slavs! . . . But you are not listening. Do you know, you are not at all well this evening? I know you went yesterday to that doctor . . . well, what about your health? What did the doctor say?''

"Fool!" Ivan snapped out.

"But you — you are clever, anyway. Are you berating me again? I didn't ask out of sympathy. You needn't answer. Now rheumatism has come in again . . ."

"Fool!" repeated Ivan.

"You keep saying the same thing; but I had such an attack of rheumatism last year that I remember it to this day."

"The devil have rheumatism!"

"Why not, if I sometimes put on human form? I put it on and I take the consequences. I am Satan, and nothing that is human seems strange to me."

"What, what? 'I am Satan and nothing that is human' . . . That's not bad for the devil!"

"I am glad I've pleased you at last."

"But you didn't get that from me," Ivan stopped suddenly, seeming struck. "That never entered my head, that's strange."

"It's original, isn't it? This time I'll act honestly and explain to you. Listen, in dreams and especially in nightmares, from indigestion or anything, a man sometimes sees such artistic visions, such complex reality, even a whole world of events, woven into a plot with such unexpected details from the most exalted matters to the last button on a cuff, as I swear Leo Tolstoy has never invented. Yet such dreams are sometimes seen not by writers, but by the most ordinary people, officials, journalists, priests . . . The subject is a complete enigma. Indeed, a statesman confessed to me that all his best ideas came to him when he was asleep. Well, that's how it is now — though I am your hallucination, yet just as in a nightmare, I say original things that had not entered your head before. So I don't repeat your ideas; yet I am only your nightmare, nothing more."

"You are lying, your aim is to convince me you exist apart from me and are not my nightmare, and now you are asserting you are a dream."

"My dear fellow, I've adopted a special method today, I'll explain it to you afterwards. Stay, where did I break off? Oh, yes! I caught cold then, only not here but yonder."

"Where is yonder? Tell me, will you be here long? Can't you go away?" Ivan exclaimed almost in despair! He ceased walking to and fro, sat down on the sofa, leaned his elbows on the table again and held his head tight in both hands. He pulled the wet towel off and flung it away in vexation. It was evidently of no use.

"Your nerves are out of order," observed the gentleman, with a carelessly easy, though perfectly polite, air. "You are angry with me even for being able to catch cold, though it happened in a most natural way. I was hurrying then to a diplomatic soirée at the house of a lady of high rank in Petersburg, who was aiming at influence in the Ministry. Well, of course an evening suit, white tie, gloves, though I was God knows where and had to fly through space to reach your earth . . . Of course, it took only an instant, but you know a ray of light from the sun takes fully eight minutes, and fancy! — in an evening suit and open waistcoat. Spirits don't freeze, but when one's in human form, well . . . in brief, I didn't think and set off, and you know in those ethereal spaces, in the water that is above the firmament, there's such a frost . . . one can't call it mere frost, just fancy, 150° below zero! You know the game the village girls play — they invite the unwary to lick an axe in thirty degrees below zero; the tongue instantly freezes to it, and the stupid fellow jerks his tongue away, torn and bleeding. But that's only in 30°, in 150° I imagine it would be enough to put your finger on the axe for it to be the end of it . . . if that is, there could be an axe there."

"And can there be an axe there?" Ivan interrupted, carelessly and disdainfully. He was exerting himself to the utmost not to believe in the delusion and not to sink into complete insanity.

"An axe?" the guest interrupted in surprise.

"Yes, what would become of an axe there?" Ivan cried suddenly, with a sort of savage and insistent obstinacy.

"What would become of an axe in space? What an idea! If it were to fall to any distance, it would begin, I think, flying round the earth without knowing why, like a satellite. The astronomers would calculate the rising and the setting of the axe, Gatzuk would put it in his calendar, that's all."

"You are stupid, awfully stupid," said Ivan peevishly. "Lie more cleverly or I won't listen. You want to get the better of me by realism, to convince me that you exist, but I don't want to believe you exist! I won't believe it!"

"But I am not lying, it's all the truth; the truth is unhappily hardly ever amusing. I see you persist in expecting something big of me and perhaps something fine. That's a great pity, for I only give what I can . . ."

"Don't talk philosophy, you ass!"

"Philosophy, indeed, when all my right side is numb and I am moaning and groaning. I've tried all kinds of doctors; they can diagnose beautifully, they have the whole of your disease at their finger–tips, but they've no idea how to cure you. There was an enthusiastic little student here, 'You may die,' said he, 'but you'll at least know perfectly well what disease you are dying of!' And then what a way they have of sending people to specialists. 'We only diagnose,' they say, 'but go to such and such a specialist; he'll cure you.' The old doctor who used to cure all sorts of diseases has completely disappeared, I assure you; now there are only specialists and they all advertise in newspapers. If anything is wrong with your nose, they send you to Paris — there, they say, is a European specialist who cures noses. If you go to Paris, he'll look at your nose; 'I can only cure your right nostril,' he'll tell you, 'for I don't cure the left nostril, that's not my speciality, but go to Vienna where a specialist will cure your left nostril.' What are you to do? I returned to popular remedies; a German doctor advised me to rub myself with honey and salt in the bath-house. Just to get an extra bath I went, smeared myself all over, and it did me no good at all. In despair I wrote to Count Mattei in Milan. He sent me a book and some drops, bless him, and only fancy, Hoff's malt extract cured me! I bought it by accident, drank a bottle and a half of it, and I was ready to dance; it took it away completely. I made up my mind to write to the papers to thank him; I was prompted by a feeling of gratitude, and it led to no end of a bother: not a single paper would take my letter. 'It would be very reactionary;' they said, 'no one will believe it. The devil simply doesn't exist. You'd better remain anonymous.' What use is a letter of thanks if it's anonymous? I laughed with the men at the newspaper office; 'It's reactionary to believe in God in our days,' I said, 'but I am the devil, so I may be believed in.' 'We quite understand that,' they said. 'Who doesn't believe in the devil? Yet it won't do, it might injure our reputation. As a joke, if you like.' But I thought as a joke it wouldn't be very witty. So it wasn't printed. And do you know, I have felt sore about it to this day. My best feelings, gratitude for instance, are literally denied me simply from my social position.''

"Philosophical reflections again?'' Ivan snarled malignantly.

"God preserve me from it, but one can't help complaining sometimes. I am a slandered man. You upbraid me every moment with being stupid. One can see you are young. My dear fellow, intelligence isn't the only thing! I have a naturally kind and merry heart. I also write comic theatricals of all sorts. You seem to take me for Hlestakov grown old, but my fate is a far more serious one. Before time was, by some decree which I could never make out, I was predestined 'to deny' and yet I am genuinely good-hearted and not at all inclined to negation. No, you must go and negate; without negation there's no criticism and what would a journal be without a column of criticism? Without criticism it would be nothing but one 'hosannah.' But hosannah alone is not enough for life; this hosannah must be tried in the crucible of doubt and so on, in the same vein. But I don't meddle in that, I didn't create it, I am not answerable for it. Well, they've chosen their scapegoat, they've made me write the column of criticism and so life was made possible. We understand that comedy; I, for instance, simply ask for annihilation. No, I am told, live, for there'd be nothing without you. If everything in the universe were sensible, nothing would happen. There would be no events without you, and there must be events. So against the grain, I serve to produce events and do what's irrational because I am commanded to. For all their indisputable intelligence, men take this farce as something serious and that is their tragedy. They suffer, of course . . . but they live; they live a real life, not one of fantasy, for suffering is life. Without suffering what would be the pleasure of it? It would be transformed into an endless church service; it would be holy, but tedious. But what about me? I suffer but still don't live. I am x in an indeterminate equation. I am a sort of phantom in life who has lost all beginning and end and who has even forgotten his own name. You are laughing — no, you are not laughing, you are angry again. You are forever angry, all you care about is intelligence, but I repeat again that I would give away all this superstellar life, all the ranks and honors, simply to be transformed into the soul of a merchant's wife weighing 250 pounds, setting candles at God's shrine.''

"Then even you don't believe in God?'' said Ivan, with a smile of hatred.

"What can I say — that is, if you are in earnest . . .''

"Is there a God or not?'' Ivan cried with the same savage intensity.

"Ah, then you are in earnest! My dear fellow, upon my word I don't know. There! I've said it now!''

"You don't know, but you see God? No, you are not someone apart, you are myself, you are I and nothing more! You are rubbish, you are my fancy!''

"Well, if you like, I have the same philosophy as you, that would be true. 'I think, therefore I am,' I know for a fact; all the rest, all these worlds, God and even Satan — all that is not proved to me. Does all that exist of itself, or is it only an emanation of myself, a logical development of my ego, which alone has existed forever — but I make haste to stop, for I believe you will be jumping up to beat me directly.''

"You'd better tell me some anecdote!'' said Ivan miserably.

"There is an anecdote precisely on our subject, or rather a legend, not an anecdote. You reproach me with unbelief: 'You see,' you say, 'yet you don't believe.' But, my dear fellow, I am not the only one like that. We are all in a muddle over there now, and all through your science. Once there used to be atoms, five senses, and four elements, and then everything hung together somehow. There were atoms even in the ancient world, but since you've discovered the chemical molecule and protoplasm and the devil knows what, we had to pull in our horns, so to speak. There's a regular muddle, and above all, superstition and scandal; there's as much scandal among us as among you, you know; a little more in fact, even denouncements, for we have our secret police where informers are received. Well, this wild legend belongs to our middle ages — not yours but ours — and no one believes it even among us, except the old 250-pound wives, not your old wives but ours. We've everything you have; I am revealing one of our secrets out of friendship for you, though it's forbidden. This legend is about Paradise. There was, they say, here on earth a thinker and philosopher. He rejected everything, 'laws, conscience, faith,' and above all, the future life. He died; he expected to go straight to darkness and death, and he found a future life before him. He was astounded and indignant. 'This is against my principles!' he said. And he was punished for that . . . that is, you must excuse me, I am just repeating what I heard myself, it's only a legend . . . he was sentenced to walk a quadrillion kilometres in the dark (we've adopted the metric system, you know) and when he has finished that quadrillion, the gates of heaven would be opened to him and he'll be forgiven . . .''

"And what tortures have you in the other world besides the quadrillion kilometres?" asked Ivan with a strange eagerness.

"What tortures? Ah, don't ask. In the old days we had all sorts, but now they have taken chiefly to moral punishments — 'the stings of conscience' and all that nonsense. We got that too from you, from the softening of your manners. And who's the better for it? Only those who have no conscience, for how can they be tortured by conscience when they have none? But decent people who have a conscience and a sense of honor suffer for it. Reforms — when the ground has not been prepared for them, and especially if they are institutions copied from abroad — do nothing but mischief! The ancient fire was better. Well, this man who was condemned to the quadrillion kilometres stood still, looked round, and lay down across the road. 'I won't go, I refuse on principle!' Take the soul of an enlightened Russian atheist and mix it with the soul of the prophet Jonah, who sulked for three days and nights in the belly of the whale, and you get the character of that thinker who lay across the road.''

"What did he lie on there?''

"Well, I suppose there was something to lie on. You are not laughing?''

"Bravo!'' cried Ivan, still with the same strange eagerness. Now he was listening with an unexpected curiosity. "Well, is he lying there now?''

"That's the point, he isn't. He lay there almost a thousand years, and then he got up and went on.''

"What an ass!'' cried Ivan, laughing nervously and still seeming to be pondering something intently. "Does it make any difference whether he lies there forever or walks the quadrillion kilometres? It would take a billion years to walk it?''

"Much more than that. I haven't got a pencil and paper or I could work it out. But he got there long ago and that's where the story begins.''

"What, he got there? But how did he get the billion years to do it?''

"Why, you keep thinking of our present earth! But our present earth may have been repeated a billion times. Why, it's become extinct, been frozen; cracked, broken to bits, disintegrated into its elements, again 'the water above the firmament,' then again a comet, again a sun, again from the sun it becomes earth — and the same sequence may have been repeated endlessly and exactly the same to every detail, most unseemly and insufferably tedious . . ."

"Well, well, what happened when he arrived?"

"Why, the moment the gates of Paradise were open and he walked in, before he had been there two seconds by his watch (though to my thinking his watch must have long dissolved into its elements on the way), he cried out that those two seconds were worth walking not a quadrillion kilometres but a quadrillion of quadrillions, raised to the quadrillionth power! In fact, he sang 'hosannah' and overdid it so that some persons of lofty ideas wouldn't shake hands with him at first — he'd gone over to the conservatives too eagerly, they said. The Russian temperament, I repeat, is a legend. I give it you for what it's worth. So that's the sort of ideas we have on such subjects even now."

"I've caught you!" Ivan cried, with an almost childish delight, as though he had succeeded in remembering something at last. "That anecdote about the quadrillion years, I made up myself! I was seventeen then, I was at the high school. I made up that anecdote and told it to a schoolfellow called Korovkin. It was in Moscow . . . The anecdote is so characteristic that I couldn't have taken it from anywhere. I thought I'd forgotten it . . . but I've unconsciously recalled it — I recalled it myself — it was not you telling it! Thousands of things are unconsciously remembered like that even when people are being taken to execution . . . it's come back to me in a dream. You are that dream! You are a dream, not a living creature!"

"From the vehemence with which you deny my existence," laughed the gentleman, "I am convinced that you believe in me."

"Not in the slightest! I haven't a hundredth part of a grain of faith in you!"

"But you have the thousandth of a grain. Homeopathic doses perhaps are the strongest. Confess that you have faith even to the ten-thousandth of a grain."

"Not for one minute," cried Ivan furiously. "But I should like to believe in you," he added strangely.

"Aha! There's an admission! But I am good-natured. I'll come to your assistance again. Listen, it was I caught you, not you me. I told you your anecdote you'd forgotten, on purpose, so as to destroy your faith in me completely."

"You are lying. The object of your visit is to convince me of your existence!"

"Just so. But hesitation, suspense, conflict between belief and disbelief — is sometimes such torture to a conscientious man like you that it's better to hang oneself at once. Knowing that you are inclined to believe in me, I administered some disbelief by telling you that anecdote. I lead you to belief and disbelief by turns, and I have my motive in it. It's the new method. As soon as you disbelieve in me completely, you'll begin assuring me that I am not a dream but a reality. I know you. Then I shall have attained my object, which is an honorable one. I shall sow in you only a tiny grain of faith and it will grow into an oak tree — and such an oak tree that, sitting on it, you will long to enter the ranks of 'the hermits in the wilderness and the saintly women,' for that is what you are secretly longing for. You'll dine on locusts, you'll wander into the wilderness to save your soul!"

"Then it's for the salvation of my soul you are working, is it, you scoundrel?"

"One must do a good work sometimes. How ill-humored you are!"

"Fool! did you ever tempt those holy men who ate locusts and prayed seventeen years in the wilderness till they were overgrown with moss?"

"My dear fellow, I've done nothing else. One forgets the

whole world and all the worlds, and sticks to one such saint, because he is a very precious diamond. One such soul, you know, is sometimes worth a whole constellation. We have our system of reckoning, you know. The conquest is priceless! And some of them, on my word, are not inferior to you in culture, though you won't believe it. They can contemplate such depths of belief and disbelief at the same moment that sometimes it really seems that they are within a hair's-breadth of being 'turned topsy-turvy,' as the actor Gorbunov says."

"Well, did you get your nose pulled out of joint?"

"My dear fellow," observed the visitor sententiously, "it's better to get off with your nose pulled than with no nose at all, as an afflicted marquis (he must have been treated by a specialist) observed not long ago in confession to his spiritual father, a Jesuit. I was present, it was simply charming. 'Give me back my nose!' he said, and he beat his breast. 'My son,' said the priest evasively, 'all things are accomplished in accordance with the inscrutable decrees of Providence, and what seems a misfortune sometimes leads to extraordinary, though unapparent, benefits. If stern destiny has deprived you of your nose, it's to your advantage that no one can ever pull it again. 'Holy father, that's no comfort,' cried the despairing marquis. 'I'd be delighted to have my nose pulled every day of my life, if it were only in its proper place.' 'My son,' sighs the priest, 'you can't expect every blessing at once. This is murmuring against Providence, who even in this has not forgotten you, for if you repine as you repined just now, declaring you'd be glad to have your nose pulled for the rest of your life, your desire has already been fulfilled indirectly, for when you lost your nose, you were pulled by the nose.'"

"Phooey, how stupid!" cried Ivan.

"My dear friend, I only wanted to amuse you. But I swear that's the genuine Jesuit casuistry, and I swear that it all happened word for word as I've told you. It happened lately and gave me a great deal of trouble. The unhappy young man shot himself that very night when he got home. I was by his side till the very last moment. Those Jesuit confessionals are really my most delightful diversion at melancholy moments. Here's another incident that happened only the other day. A little blond Norman girl of twenty — a buxom, unsophisticated beauty that would make your mouth water — comes to an old priest. She bends down and whispers her sin into the grating. 'Why, my daughter, have you fallen again already?' cries the priest. 'O Sancta Maria, what do I hear! Not the same man this time, how long is this going on? Aren't you ashamed!' 'O father,' answers the sinner with tears of penitence, 'it gives him so much pleasure with so little pain to me!' Fancy such an answer! I drew back. It was the cry of nature, and if you like, better than innocence itself. I absolved her sin on the spot and was turning to go, but I was forced to turn back. I heard the priest at the grating making an appointment with her for the evening — though he was an old man and hard as flint, he fell in an instant! It was nature, the truth of nature asserting its rights! What, you are turning up your nose again? Angry again? I don't know how to please you . . .''

Leave me alone, you are beating on my brain like a haunting nightmare,'' Ivan moaned miserably, helpless before his apparition. ''I am bored with you, agonizingly and insufferably. I would give anything to be able to shake you off!''

''I repeat, moderate your expectations, don't demand of me 'everything great and noble' and you'll see how well we shall get on,'' said the gentleman impressively. ''You are really angry with me for not having appeared to you in a red glow, with thunder and lightning and with scorched wings, but have shown myself in such a modest form. You are wounded, in the first place in your aesthetic feelings, and secondly in your pride. How could such a vulgar devil visit such a great man as you! Yes, there is that romantic strain in you that was so derided by Belinsky. I can't help it, young man, as I got ready to come to you I did think of appearing as a joke in the figure of a retired general who had served in the Caucasus, with a star of the Lion and the Sun on my coat. But I was positively afraid of doing it, for you'd have thrashed me for daring to pin the Lion and the Sun on my coat instead of at least the Polar Star or Sirius. And you keep on saying I am stupid, but mercy on us, I make no claim to be equal to you in intelligence! Mephistopheles declared to Faust that he desired evil but did only good. Well, he can say what he likes, it's quite the opposite with me. I am perhaps the one man in all creation who loves the truth and genuinely desires good. I was there when the Word, Who died on the Cross, rose up into Heaven bearing on His bosom the soul of the penitent thief. I heard the glad shrieks of the cherubim singing and shouting hosannah and the thunderous rapture of the seraphim which shook heaven and all creation, and I swear to you by all that's sacred, I longed to join the choir and shout hosannah with them all. The word had almost escaped me, had almost broken from my lips — you know how susceptible and aesthetically impressionable I am. But common sense — oh, a most unhappy trait in my character — kept me in due bounds and I let the moment pass! For what would have happened, I reflected, what would have happened after my hosannah? Everything on earth would have been extinguished at once and then no more events could have occurred. And so solely from a sense of duty and my social position, I was forced to suppress the good moment and stick to my nasty task. Somebody else takes all the credit for what's good, and nothing but nastiness is left for me. But I don't envy the honor of a life of idle imposture; I am not ambitious. Why am I, of all creatures in the world, doomed to be cursed by all decent people and even to be kicked, for if I put on mortal form I am bound to take such consequences sometimes? I know, of course, there's a secret in it, but they won't tell me the secret for anything, for then perhaps, seeing the meaning of it, I might bawl hosannah, and the indispensable minus would disappear at once, and good sense would reign supreme throughout the whole world. And that, of course, would mean the end of everything, even of magazines and newspapers, for who would take them in? I know that at the end of all things I shall be reconciled. I too shall walk my quadrillion and learn the secret. But till that happens I am sulking and fulfilling my destiny, though it's against the grain — that is, to ruin thousands for the sake of saving one. How many souls have had to be ruined and how many honorable reputations destroyed for the sake of that one righteous man Job, over whom they made such a fool of me in old days. Yes, till the secret is revealed, there are two sorts of truth for me — one, their truth yonder which I know nothing about so far and the other, my own. And there's no knowing which will turn out the better . . . Are you asleep?"

"I might well be," Ivan groaned angrily. "All my stupid ideas — outgrown, thrashed out long ago, and flung aside like a dead carcass — you present to me as something new!"

"There's no pleasing you! And I thought I should fascinate you by my literary style. That hosannah in the skies really wasn't bad, was it? And that ironical tone á la Heine, eh?"

"No, I was never such a flunkey! How then could my soul beget a flunkey like you?"

"My dear fellow, I know a most charming and attractive young Russian gentleman, a young thinker and a great lover of literature and art, the author of a promising poem entitled 'The Grand Inquisitor.' I was only thinking of him!"

"I forbid you to speak of 'The Grand Inquisitor,'" cried Ivan, crimson with shame.

"And the 'Geological Cataclysm.' Do you remember? That was a poem, now!"

"Hold your tongue, or I'll kill you!"

"You'll kill me? No, excuse me, I will speak. I came to treat myself to that pleasure. Oh, I love the dreams of my ardent young friends, quivering with eagerness for life! 'There are new men,' you decided last spring, when you were meaning to come here. 'They propose to destroy everything and begin with cannibalism. Stupid fellows! They didn't ask my advice! I maintain that nothing need be destroyed, that we only need to destroy the idea of God in man, that's how we have to set to work. That is what we must begin with. Oh, blind race of men who have no understanding! As soon as men, all of them, have denied God — and I believe that period, analogous to geological periods, will come to pass — the old conception of the universe will fall of itself — without cannibalism — and what's more the old morality, and everything will begin anew. Men will unite to take from life all it can give, but only for joy and happiness in the present world. Man will be lifted up with a spirit of divine titanic pride and the man-god will appear. Extending his conquest of nature infinitely from hour to hour by his will and his science, man will feel hourly such lofty joy in doing it that it will make up for all his old dreams of the joys of heaven. Every one will know that he is mortal and will accept death proudly and serenely like a god. His pride will teach him that it's useless for him to repine over life's being but a moment, and he will love his brother without need of reward. Love will be sufficient even for a moment of life, but the very consciousness of its momentariness will intensify its fire, which now is dissipated in dreams of eternal love beyond the grave . . . and so on and so on in the same vein. Charming!"

Ivan sat with his eyes on the floor and his hands pressed

to his ears, but he began trembling all over. The voice continued.

"The question now is, my young thinker reflected, is it possible that such a period will ever come? If it does, everything is determined and humanity is settled for ever. But since, owing to man's inveterate stupidity, this cannot come about for at least a thousand years, every one who recognizes the truth even now may legitimately order his life as he pleases, on the new principles. In that sense 'All things are lawful' for him. What's more, even if this period never comes to pass, since there is anyway no God and no immortality, the new man may well become the man–god, even if he is the only one in the whole world, and promoted to his new position, he may if necessary, lightheartedly overstep all the barriers of the slave–man's old morality. There is no law for God. Where God stands, the place is holy. Where I stand is at once the foremost place where 'all things are lawful' — and that's the end of it! That's all very charming, but if you want to swindle why do you want a moral sanction for doing it? That's our modern Russian all over. He can't bring himself to swindle without a moral sanction. He is so in love with truth . . .''

The visitor talked, obviously carried away by his own eloquence, speaking louder and louder and looking ironically at his host. But he did not succeed in finishing; Ivan suddenly snatched a glass from the table and flung it at the orator.

"But how stupid!" cried the latter, jumping up from the sofa and shaking the drops of tea off himself. "He remembers Luther's inkstand! He takes me for a dream and throws glasses at a dream! It's like a woman! I suspected you were only pretending to stop up your ears."

A loud persistent knocking was suddenly heard at the window. Ivan jumped up from the sofa.

The Failure of Christendom

Toward the end of the novel The Idiot, *Prince Myshkin is being introduced (to a party in high society at the home of General Epanchin) as the possible fiancé of the youngest Epanchin daughter, Aglaia. Unexpectedly, Myshkin hears of the conversion to Roman Catholicism of his guardian and protector, Nickolay Andreyevitch Pavlishtchev. Myshkin's outburst against Roman Catholicism comes as an embarrassment to the respectable gathering but is laughed off when he breaks an enormous china vase.*

This passage reflects Prince Myshkin's strong passion for the soul and heart of Russia. Is his indignation not a reflection on the failure of the whole of Christendom after Constantine and the third century: "universal political supremacy" grasped by "the sword" supplanting faith, "the most holy" bartered for the most unholy. Dostoyevsky's Myshkin might be grieving for the original Church of Jesus Christ set right into this world to make it a place of justice and love, the Church of Jesus' own prayer, "Thy Kingdom come, Thy will be done on earth . . . !*"*

"Pavlishtchev was a clear-headed man and a Christian, a genuine Christian," Myshkin brought out suddenly. "How could he have accepted a faith . . . that's unchristian? Catholicism is as good as an unchristian religion!" he added suddenly, looking about him with flashing eyes as though scanning the whole company.

"Come, that's too much!" muttered the old man, and he looked with surprise at General Epanchin.

"How do you mean Catholicism is an unchristian religion," said Ivan Petrovitch, turning round in his chair. "What is it then?"

"An unchristian religion in the first place!" Myshkin began, in extreme agitation and with excessive abruptness. "And in the second place Roman Catholicism is even worse than atheism itself, in my opinion! Yes, that's my opinion! Atheism only preaches a negation, but Catholicism goes further: it preaches a distorted Christ, a Christ calumniated and defamed by it, the opposite of Christ! It preaches the Antichrist, I declare it does, I assure you it does! This is the conviction I have long held, and it has distressed me . . . Roman Catholicism cannot hold its position without universal political supremacy, and cries: 'We cannot!' To my thinking Roman Catholicism is not even a religion, but simply the continuation of the Western Roman Empire, and everything in it is subordinated to that idea — faith to begin with. The Pope seized the earth, an earthly throne, and grasped the sword; everything has gone on in the same way since, only they have added to the sword lying, fraud, deceit, fanaticism, superstition, villainy. They have trifled with the most holy, truthful, sincere, fervent feelings of the people; they have bartered it all, all for money, for base earthly power. And isn't that the teaching of Antichrist? How could atheism fail to come from them? Atheism has sprung from Roman Catholicism itself. It originated with them. Can they have believed themselves? It has been strengthened by revulsion from them; it is begotten by their lying and their spiritual impotence. Atheism! Among us it is only the exceptional classes who don't believe, those who, as Yevgeny Pavlovitch splendidly expressed it the other day, have lost their roots. But over there, in Europe, a terrible mass of the people are beginning to lose their faith — at first from darkness and lying, and now from fanaticism and hatred of the church and Christianity.''

Myshkin paused to take breath. He had been talking fearfully fast. He was pale and breathless. They all glanced at one another, and at last the old dignitary simply burst out laughing. Prince N. drew out his lorgnette and took a prolonged stare at Myshkin. The German poet crept out of his corner and moved nearer to the table with a spiteful smile on his face.

"You are exaggerating very much," Ivan Petrovitch drawled with an air of being bored, and even rather ashamed of something. "There are representatives of that Church who are virtuous and worthy of all respect . . ."

"I have said nothing about individual representatives of the Church. I was speaking of Roman Catholicism in its essence. I am speaking of Rome. Can a Church disappear altogether? I never said that!"

"I agree. But all that's well known and — irrelevant, indeed, and . . . it's a theological question . . ."

"Oh, no, no! It's not only a theological question, I assure you it's not! It concerns us much more closely than you think. That's our whole mistake, that we can't see that this is not exclusively a theological question! Why, socialism too springs from Catholicism and the Catholic idea! Like its brother atheism, it comes from despair in opposition to Catholicism on the moral side to replace the lost moral power of religion, to quench the spiritual thirst of parched humanity, and to save them not by Christ but also by violence. That too is freedom through violence, that too is union through sword and blood. 'Don't dare to believe in God, don't dare to have property and individuality, brotherhood or death, two million heads!' By their works ye shall know them — as it is said. And don't imagine that all this is so harmless and without danger for us. Oh, we need to make resistance at once, at once! Our Christ whom we have kept and they have never known must shine forth and vanquish the West. Not letting ourselves be slavishly caught by the wiles of the Jesuits, but carrying our Russian civilization to them, we ought to stand before them and not let it be said among us, as it was just now, that their preaching is skilful.''

"But allow me, allow me!'' said Ivan Petrovitch, growing dreadfully uneasy, looking about him, and positively beginning to be terrified. "All your ideas, of course, are very praiseworthy and full of patriotism, but all this is exaggerated in the extreme, and . . . in fact, we had better drop the subject . . .''

"No, it's not exaggerated; it's even understated, positively understated, because I am not capable of expressing . . .''

"Al-low me!''

Myshkin ceased speaking, and sitting upright in his chair gazed with a fixed and fervent look at Ivan Petrovitch.

"I fancy you have been too much affected by what happened to your benefactor,'' the old dignitary indulgently observed, with unruffled composure. "You have grown over ardent . . . perhaps from solitude. If you were to live more among people and to see more of the world, I expect you would be welcomed as a remarkable young man; then, of course, you would grow less excitable and you would see that it is all much simpler . . . and besides such exceptional cases are due in my opinion partly to our being blasé, partly to our being . . . bored.''

"Just so, just so!'' cried Myshkin. "A splendid idea! It's just from dullness, from our dullness. Not from being blasé. On the contrary, from unsatisfied yearning . . . not from being blasé. There you're mistaken. Not simply from unsatisfied yearnings, but from feverishness, from burning thirst. And . . . and don't think that it's to such a slight extent that one can afford to laugh at it. Excuse me, one needs to look ahead in these things. As soon as Russians feel the ground under their feet and are confident that they have reached firm ground, they are so delighted at reaching it that they rush at once to the furthest limit. Why is that? You are surprised at Pavlishtchev, and you put it down to madness on his part, or to simplicity. But it's not that! And Russian intensity in such cases is a surprise not to us only but to all Europe. If one of us turns Catholic, he is bound to become a Jesuit, and one of the most fanatical. If he becomes an atheist, he's sure to clamor for the extirpation of belief in God by force, that is, by the sword. Why is this, why such frenzy? You must surely know! Because he has found the fatherland which he has missed here. He has reached the shore, he has found the land and he rushes to kiss it.

"Russian atheists and Russian Jesuits are the outcome not only of vanity, not only of a bad, vain feeling, but also of spiritual agony, spiritual thirst, a craving for something higher, for a firm footing, for a fatherland in which they have ceased to believe, because they have never even known it! It's easier for a Russian to become an atheist than for anyone else in the world. And Russians do not merely become atheists, but they invariably *believe* in atheism, as though it were a new religion without noticing that they are putting faith in a negation. So great is our craving! 'He who has no roots beneath him has no god.' That's not my own saying. It was said by a merchant and Old Believer, whom I met when I was travelling. It's true he did not use those words. He said: 'The man who has renounced his fatherland has renounced his god.' Only think that among us, even highly educated people join the sect of Flagellants. Though why is that worse than nihilism, Jesuitism, or atheism? It may even be rather more profound! But that's what their agony has brought them to.

Reveal to the yearning and feverish companions of Columbus the 'New World,' reveal to the Russian the 'world' of Russia, let him find the gold, the treasure hidden from him in the earth! Show him the whole of humanity, rising again, and renewed by Russian thought alone, perhaps by the Russian God and Christ, and you will see into what a mighty and truthful, what a wise and gentle giant he will grow, before the eyes of the astounded world — astounded and dismayed, because it expects of us nothing but the sword, nothing but the sword and violence, because, judging us by themselves, the other peoples cannot picture us free from barbarism. That has always been so hitherto and goes on getting more so!''

ON THE WAY TO GOD

The Story of Marie

The story is told by Prince Myshkin in The Idiot. *The prince tells it to his new acquaintances and distant relatives, the women of the Epanchin family, who are questioning him about his past. He has just returned to Russia on business after a long period of medical treatment in Switzerland under Professor Schneider, a specialist in illnesses such as Myshkin's. Schneider had taken over full responsibility for him after his benefactor Pavlishtchev's death two years earlier. The story of the tragic Marie and the children reveals Myshkin's character — his love quietly accepts ridicule and the taunt of idiot.*

"Very well," Adelaïda interposed hurriedly again, "but if you are such an expert on faces, you certainly must have been in love . . . Tell us about it."

"I haven't been in love," answered Myshkin as gently and gravely as before. "I . . . have been happy in a different way."

"How? In what?"

"Very well, I'll tell you," said Myshkin, as though meditating profoundly.

"You are all looking at me with such curiosity," began Myshkin, "that if I didn't satisfy it you might be angry with me. No, I am joking," he added quickly, with a smile. "There were lots of children there, and I was always with the children, only with the children. They were the children of the village, a

89

whole crowd of schoolchildren. It was not that I taught them. Oh, no, there was a schoolmaster for that — Jules Thibaut. Perhaps I did teach them too, but for the most part I was simply with them, and all those four years were spent in their company. I wanted nothing else. I used to tell them everything; I concealed nothing from them. Their fathers and relations were all cross with me, for finally the children couldn't get on without me and were always flocking round me, and at the end the schoolmaster became my chief enemy. I made many enemies there, and all on account of the children. Even Schneider reproved me. And what were they afraid of? Children can be told anything — anything. I've always been struck by seeing what little understanding grown-up people have for children, how little even parents understand their own children. Nothing should be concealed from children on the pretext that they are little and that it is too early for them to understand. What a miserable and unfortunate idea! And how readily the children detect that their fathers consider them too little to understand anything, though they understand everything. Grown-up people do not know that a child can give exceedingly good advice even in the most difficult case. Oh, dear! when that pretty little bird looks at you, happy and confiding, it's a shame for you to deceive it. I call them birds because there's nothing better than a bird in the world.

"What really set all the village against me was something that happened . . . but Thibaut was simply envious of me. At first he used to shake his head and wonder how it was the children understood everything from me and scarcely anything from him; and then he began laughing at me when I told him that neither of us could teach them anything, but that they can teach us. And how could he be envious of me and say things against me, when he spent his life with children himself! The soul is healed by being with children . . . There was one patient in Schneider's institution, a very unhappy man. I doubt whether there could be any unhappiness equal to his. He was there to be treated for insanity. In my opinion he was not mad, simply frightfully miserable; that was all that was the matter with him. And if only you knew what our children were to him in the end . . . But I'd better tell you about that patient another time. I'll tell you now how it all began. At first the children didn't take to me. I was so big, I am always so clumsy; I know I am ugly too . . . and then I was a foreigner. The children used to laugh at me at first, and they began throwing stones at me after they saw me kiss Marie. And I only kissed her once . . . No, don't laugh.'' Myshkin made haste to check the smile on the faces of his listeners. "It was not a question of love. If only you knew what an unhappy being she was, you would be very sorry for her, as I was.

"She lived in our village. Her mother was an old woman. One of the two windows of their tumble-down little house was set apart, by permission of the village authorities, and from it the old woman was allowed to sell laces, thread, tobacco and soap. It all came to a few halfpence and that was what she lived on. She was an invalid; her legs were all swollen so that she could not move from her seat. Marie was her daughter, a girl of twenty, weak and thin. She had been consumptive for a long time, but she went from house to house doing hard work — scrubbing floors, washing, sweeping out yards and minding cattle. A French commercial traveller seduced her and took her away, and a week later deserted her and went off on the sly. She made her way home begging, all mud-stained and in rags, with her shoes coming to pieces. She was a week walking back, had spent the nights in the fields and caught a fearful cold. Her feet were covered with sores, her hands were chapped and swollen. She wasn't pretty before, though; only her eyes were gentle, kind and innocent. She was extremely silent. Once when she was at work she began singing, and I remember everyone was surprised and began laughing. 'Marie singing! What, Marie singing!' She was fearfully abashed and did not open her lips again. In those days, people were still kind to her, but when she came back broken down and ill, no one had any sympathy for her. How cruel people are in that way! What hard ideas they have about such things! Her mother, to begin with, received her with anger and contempt: 'You have disgraced me!' She was the first to abandon her to shame. As soon as they heard in the village that Marie had come home, every one went to have a look at her, and almost all the village assembled in the old woman's cottage — old men, children, women, girls, everyone — an eager, hurrying crowd. Marie was lying on the ground at the old woman's feet, hungry and in rags, and she was weeping. When they all ran in, she hid her face in her disheveled hair and lay face downward on the floor. They all stared at her, as though she were a reptile; the old people blamed and upbraided her, the young people laughed; the women reviled and abused her and looked at her with loathing, as though she had been a spider. Her mother allowed it all; she sat there nodding her head and approving. The mother was very ill at the time and almost dying: two months later she did die. She knew she was dying, but up to the time of her death she didn't dream of being reconciled to her daughter. She didn't speak one word to her, turned her out to sleep in the entry, scarcely gave her anything to eat. Her bad legs had to be bathed constantly in hot water. Marie bathed her legs every day and waited on her. She accepted all her services in silence and never said a kind word to her. Marie put up with everything, and afterward when I made her acquaintance, I noticed that she thought it all right and looked on herself as the lowest of the low. When the old mother was completely bedridden, the old women of the village came to sit up with her in turns, as their custom is. Then they gave up feeding Marie altogether, and in the village every one drove her away and no one would even give her work as before. Every one, as it were, spat on her, and the men no longer looked on her as a woman even; they would say all sorts of nasty things to her. Sometimes, though not often, when the men got drunk on Sunday, they would amuse themselves by throwing farthings to her, just flinging them on the ground. Marie would pick them up without a word. She had begun to spit blood by that time. At last her clothes were in absolute tatters, so that she was ashamed to show herself in the village. She had gone barefoot since she came back.

"Then the children particularly, the whole troop of them — there were about forty schoolchildren — began jeering, and even throwing dirt at her. She asked the cowherd to let her look after the cows, but he drove her away. Then she began going off for the whole day with the flock of her own accord, without permission. As she was of great use to the cowherd and he noticed it, he no longer drove her away, and sometimes even gave her what was left from his dinner of bread and cheese. He looked upon this as a great kindness on his part. When her mother died, the pastor did not scruple to heap shame on Marie in church before all the people. Marie stood crying by the coffin as she was, in her rags. A crowd of people had collected to look at her standing by the coffin and crying. Then the pastor — he was a young man, and his whole ambition was to become a great preacher — pointed to Marie and addressing them all said, 'Here you see the cause of this worthy woman's death' (And it was not true, for the woman had been ill for two years); 'Here she stands before you and dares not look at you, for she has been marked out by the finger of God; here she is, barefoot and ragged — a warning to all who lose their virtue! Who is she? Her daughter!' and so on in the same manner. And would you believe it, this infamy pleased almost every one! But . . . then things took a different turn. The children took a line of their own, for by then they were all on my side, and had begun to love Marie.

"This was how it happened . . . I wanted to do something for Marie. She was badly in want of money, but I never had a farthing at that time. I had a little diamond pin, and I sold it to a pedlar who went from village to village buying and selling old clothes. He gave me eight francs; it was certainly worth forty. I was a long time trying to meet Marie alone. At last we met by a hedge outside the village, on a bypath to the mountain, behind a tree. Then I gave her the eight francs and told her to take care of it, because I should have no more. Then I kissed her and said that she mustn't think I had any evil intent, and that I kissed her not because I was in love with her, but because I was very sorry for her, and that I had never, from the very beginning, thought of her as guilty but only as unhappy. I wanted very much to comfort her and to persuade her that she shouldn't consider herself below everyone, but I think she didn't understand. I saw that at once, though she scarcely spoke all the time and stood before me looking down and horribly abashed. When I finished, she kissed my hand, and I at once took her hand and would have kissed it, but she pulled it away. It was then the children saw us, the whole lot of them. I learnt afterwards that they had been keeping watch on me for some time. They began whistling, clapping their hands, and laughing, and Marie ran away. I tried to speak to them, but they began throwing stones at me.

"The same day every one knew of it, the whole village. The whole brunt of it fell on Marie again; they began to dislike her more than ever. I even heard that they wanted to have her punished by the authorities, but thank goodness, that didn't come off. But the children gave her no peace: they teased her more than ever and threw dirt at her; they chased her, she ran away from them, she with her weak lungs, panting and gasping for breath. They still ran after her, shouting and reviling her. Once I positively had a fight with them. Then I began talking to them; I talked to them every day as much as I could. They sometimes stopped and listened, though they still abused me. I told them how unhappy Marie was; soon they left off abusing me and walked away in silence. Little by little, we began talking together. I concealed nothing from them; I told them the whole story. They listened with great interest and soon began to be sorry for Marie. Some of them greeted her in a friendly way when they met. It's the custom there when you meet people, whether you know them or not, to bow and wish them good-morning. I can fancy how astonished Marie was. One day two little girls got some things to eat and gave them to her; they came and told me of it. They told me that Marie cried, and that now they loved her very much. Soon all of them began to love her, and at the same time they began to love me too. They took to coming to see me often and always asked me to tell them stories. I think I must have told them well, for they were very fond of listening to me. And afterwards I read and studied simply to have things to tell them, and for the remaining three years I used to tell them stories.

"Later on, when everybody blamed me — and even Schneider — for talking to them like grown-up people and concealing nothing from them, I said that it was a shame to deceive them; that they understood everything anyway, however much things were concealed from them, and that perhaps they learned it in a bad way, but not so from me. One need only remember one's own childhood. They did not agree . . . I kissed Marie a fortnight before her mother died; by the time the pastor delivered his harangue, all the children had come over to my side. I at once told them of the pastor's action and explained it to them. They were all angry with him, and some of them were so enraged that they threw stones and broke his windows. I stopped them, for that was wrong; but every one in the village heard of it at once, and they began to accuse me of corrupting the children. Then they all realized that the children loved Marie, and were dreadfully horrified; but Marie was happy. The children were forbidden to meet her, but they ran out to where she kept the herds, nearly half a mile from the village. They carried her dainties, and some simply ran out to hug and kiss her and say 'I love you, Marie,' and then ran back as fast their legs would carry them. Marie was almost beside herself at such unlooked-for happiness; she had never dreamed of the possibility of it. She was shamefaced and joyful. What the children liked doing most, especially the girls, was running to tell her that I loved her and had talked to them a great deal about her. They told her that I told them all about her, and that now they loved her and pitied her and always would feel the same. Then they would run to me and with such joyful, busy faces tell me that they had just seen Marie and that Marie sent her greetings to me. In the evenings I used to walk to the waterfall; there was one spot there quite hidden from the village and surrounded by poplars. There they would gather round me in the evening, some even coming secretly. I think they got immense enjoyment out of my love for Marie, and that was the only point in which I deceived them. I didn't tell them that they were mistaken, that I was not in love with Marie but simply very sorry for her. I saw that they wanted to have it as they imagined and had settled among themselves, and so I said nothing and let it seem that they guessed right.

"What delicacy and tenderness were shown by those little hearts! They couldn't bear to think that while their dear Léon loved Marie she should be so badly dressed and without shoes. Would you believe it, they managed to get her shoes and stockings and linen and even a dress of some sort. How they managed to do it I can't make out. The whole troop worked. When I questioned them, they only laughed merrily, and the girls clapped their hands and kissed me. I too sometimes went to see Marie secretly. She was by that time very ill and could scarcely walk. In the end she gave up working for the herdsman, but still she went out every morning with the cattle. She used to sit a little apart. There was a ledge jutting out in an overhanging, almost vertical rock there. She used to sit on the stone out of sight, right in the corner, and she sat there almost without moving all day, from early morning till the cattle went home. By then she was so weak from consumption that she sat most of the time with her eyes shut and her head leaning against the rock, dozing and breathing painfully. Her face was as thin as a skeleton's, and the sweat stood out on her brow and temples. That was how I always found her. I used to come for a moment, and I too did not want to be seen. As soon as I appeared, Marie would start, open her eyes, and fall to kissing my hands. I no longer tried to take them away, for it was a happiness to her. All the while I sat with her she trembled and wept. She did indeed try sometimes to speak, but it was difficult to understand her. She seemed like a crazed creature in terrible excitement and delight. Sometimes the children came with me. At such times they generally stood a little way off and kept watch to protect us from anyone or anything, and that was an extraordinary pleasure to them. When we went away, Marie was again left alone with her eyes shut and her head leaning against the rock, dreaming perhaps of something.

"One morning she could no longer go out with the cows and remained at home in her deserted cottage. The children heard of it at once, and almost all of them went to ask after her that day. She lay in bed, entirely alone. For two days she was tended only by the children, who ran in to her by turns; but when the news reached the village that Marie was really dying, the old women went to sit with her and look after her. I think the villagers had begun to pity Marie; anyway, they left off scolding the children and preventing them from seeing her, as they had done before. Marie was drowsy all the time, but her sleep was broken — she coughed terribly. The old women drove the children away, but they ran under the window sometimes only for a moment, just to say, 'Good day, our dear Marie.' And as soon as she caught sight of them or heard them, she seemed to revive, and regardless of the old women, she would try to raise herself on her elbow, nod to them and thank them. They used to bring her dainties as before, but she scarcely ate anything. I assure you that, thanks to them, she died almost happy. Thanks to them, she forgot her bitter trouble; they brought her, as it were, forgiveness, for up to the very end she looked upon herself as a great sinner. They were like birds beating their wings against her window and calling to her every morning, 'We love you, Marie.'

"She died very soon. I had expected her to last much longer. The day before her death I went to her at sunset; I think she knew me, and I pressed her hand for the last time. How wasted it was! And next morning they came to me and said that Marie was dead. Then the children could not be restrained. They decked her coffin with flowers and put a wreath on her head. The pastor did no dishonor to the dead in the church. There were not many people at the funeral, only a few attracted by curiosity; but when the coffin had to be carried out, the children all rushed forward to carry it them-selves. Though they were not strong enough to bear the weight of it alone, they helped to carry it, and all ran after the coffin, crying. Marie's grave has been kept by the children ever since; they planted roses around it and deck it with flowers every year.

"But it was after the funeral that I was most persecuted by the villagers on account of the children. The pastor and the schoolmaster were at the bottom of it. The children were strictly forbidden even to meet me, and Schneider made it his duty to see that this prohibition was effectual. But we did see each other all the same; we communicated from a distance by signs. They used to send me little notes. In the end things were smoothed over; but it was very nice at that time. This persecution brought me nearer to the children than ever.

"In the last year I was almost reconciled to Thibaut and the pastor. And Schneider argued a great deal with me about my pernicious 'system' with children. As though I had a system! At last Schneider uttered a very strange thought — it was just before I went away. He told me that he had come to the conclusion that I was a complete child myself, altogether a child; that it was only in face and figure that I was like a grown-up person, but that in development, in soul, in character, and perhaps in intelligence, I was not grown up, and that so I should remain if I lived to be sixty. I laughed very much. He was wrong, of course, for I am not a child. But in one thing he is right: I don't like being with grown-up people. I've known that a long time. I don't like it because I don't know how to get on with them. Whatever they say to me, however kind they are to me, I always feel somehow oppressed with them, and I am awfully glad when I can get away to my companions; and my companions have always been children, not because I am a child myself, but simply because I always was attracted by children. When I was first in the village, at the time when I used to take melancholy walks in the mountains alone, when sometimes, especially at mid-day, I met the whole noisy troop running out of school with their satchels and slates, with shouts and games and laughter, my whole soul went out to them at once. I don't know how it was, but I had a rather intense, happy sensation at every meeting with them. I stood still and laughed with happiness, looking at their little legs forever flying along, at the boys and girls running together, at their laughter and their tears (for many of them managed to fight, cry, make it up, and begin playing again on the way home from school), and then I forgot all my mournful thoughts. For the last three years I couldn't even understand how and why people are sad. My whole life was centered on the children.

"I never planned on leaving the village, and it did not enter my mind that I should one day come back here to Russia. I thought I would always stay there. But I saw at last that Schneider couldn't go on keeping me; and then something turned up, so important apparently that Schneider himself urged me to go, and answered for me that I was coming. I shall see into it and take advice. My life will perhaps be quite changed; but that doesn't matter. What does matter is that my whole life is already changed. I left a great deal there — too much. It's all gone. As I sat in the train, I thought, 'Now I am going among people. Perhaps I know nothing, but a new life has begun for me.' I determined to do my work resolutely and honestly. I may find it dull and difficult among people. In the first place, I resolved to be courteous and open with every one. 'No one will expect more than that of me. Perhaps here too they will look on me as a child; but no matter.' Every one looks on me as an idiot for some reason. I was so ill at one time that I really was almost like an idiot. But can I be an idiot now when I am able to see for myself that people look upon me as an idiot? As I come in I think, 'I see they look upon me as an idiot, and yet I am sensible and they don't guess it.' . . . I often have that thought.

"It was only at Berlin, when I got some little letters which they had already managed to write me, that I realized how I loved the children. It's very painful getting the first letter! How distressed they were seeing me off! They'd been preparing for my going for a month beforehand. 'Léon is going away, Léon is going away, for always!' We met every evening as before at the waterfall and talked of our parting.

Sometimes we were as merry as before; only when we separated at night, they kissed and hugged me warmly, which they had not done previously. Some of them ran in secret to see me by themselves, simply to kiss and hug me alone, not before all the others. When I was setting off, the whole flock of them went with me to the station. The railway station was about a mile from our village. They tried not to cry, but some of them could not control themselves and wailed aloud, especially the girls. We made haste so as not to be late, but every now and then one of them would rush out of the crowd to throw his little arms round me and kiss me and would stop the whole procession simply for that. And although we were in a hurry, we all stopped and waited for him to say good-bye. When I'd taken my seat and the train had started, they all shouted 'Hurrah!' and stood waiting there till the train was out of sight. I gazed at them too . . ."

A Fool for Christ

In the same novel, The Idiot, *"A Fool for Christ"
describes Prince Myshkin's first meeting with Nastasya Filippovna. She arrives unexpectedly at the home of Ganya (Gavril
Ardalionovitch), who has asked her to marry him. His motive
is not love for her but of the money offered him by the wealthy
landowner Totsky. Totsky wants to free himself of her, whom
he had reared as an orphan and then had groomed to be his
mistress. Ganya's family is opposed to the match because of
her ill repute.*

*At the family gathering, among others, are Nina Alex-
androvna, Ganya's mother; Varya, his sister (fiancée of Ptitsyn, the money lender); and Kolya, his younger brother.
Ferdyshtchenko is a lodger in the house. The day is Nastasya
Filippovna's birthday, and she has promised to announce her
decision about the proposed marriage during the evening, at a
party.*

*Rogozhin is a newly rich ruffian who is insanely in love
with Nastasya Filippovna. He brings in a rowdy group of
supporters, including Lebedyev.*

*Prince Myshkin has just moved into this house as
another lodger.*

Myshkin crossed the dining room into the hall on the
way to his room. As he passed the front door, he heard and
noticed someone outside making desperate efforts to ring the
bell. But something seemed to have gone wrong with the bell;
it moved a little without making a sound. Myshkin unbolted

the door, opened it, and stepped back in amazement, startled. Nastasya Filippovna stood before him. He knew her at once from her photograph. There was a flash of annoyance in her eyes when she saw him. She walked quickly into the hall, shouldering him out of her way, and said angrily, flinging off her fur coat:

"If you are too lazy to mend the bell, you might at least be in the hall when people knock. Now he's dropped my coat, the duffer!"

The coat was indeed lying on the floor. Nastasya Filippovna, without waiting for him to help her off with it, had flung it on his arm from behind without looking, but Myshkin was not quick enough to catch it.

"They ought to turn you off. Go along and announce me."

Myshkin was about to say something, but was so abashed that he could not, and carrying the coat which he had picked up from the floor, he walked towards the drawing room.

"Well, now he is taking my coat with him! Why are you carrying my coat away? Ha, ha, ha! Are you crazy?"

Myshkin went back and stared at her, as though he were petrified. When she laughed he smiled too, but still he could not speak. At the first moment when he opened the door to her, he was pale; now the blood rushed to his face.

"What an idiot!" Nastasya Filippovna cried out, stamping her foot in indignation. "Where are you going now? What name are you going to announce?"

"Nastasya Filippovna," muttered Myshkin.

"How do you know me?" she asked him quickly. "I've never seen you. Go along, announce me. What's the shouting about in there?"

"They are quarrelling," said Myshkin, and he went into the drawing room.

He went in at a rather critical moment. Nina Alexandrovna was on the point of entirely forgetting that "she was resigned to everything"; she was defending Varya, however. Ptitsyn too was standing by Varya's side; he had left his pencilled note. Varya herself was not overawed; indeed, she was not a girl of the timid sort; but her brother's rudeness became coarser and more insufferable at every word. In such circumstances she usually left off speaking and only kept her eyes fixed on her brother in ironical silence. By this proceeding she was able, she knew, to drive her brother wild. At that moment Myshkin entered the room and announced:

"Nastasya Filippovna."

There was complete silence in the room; every one stared at Myshkin as though they didn't understand him and didn't want to understand him. Ganya was numb with horror. The arrival of Nastasya Filippovna, and especially at this juncture, was the strangest and most disturbing surprise for every one. The very fact that Nastasya Filippovna had for the first time thought fit to call on them was astounding. Hitherto she had been so haughty that she had not in talking to Ganya even expressed a desire to make the acquaintance of his family, and of late had made no allusion to them at all, as though they were nonexistent. Though Ganya was to some extent relieved at avoiding so difficult a subject, yet in his heart he treasured it up against her. In any case he would rather have expected biting and ironical remarks from her about his family than a visit to them. He knew for a fact that she was aware of all that was going on in his home in regard to his engagement and of the attitude of his family towards her. Her visit *now*, after the present of her photograph and on her birthday, the day on which she had promised to decide his fate, was almost equivalent to the decision itself.

The stupefaction with which all stared at Myshkin did

not last long. Nastasya Filippovna herself appeared at the drawing-room door and again slightly pushed him aside as she entered the room.

"At last I have managed to get in. Why do you tie up the bell?" she said good-humoredly, giving her hand to Ganya, who rushed to meet her. "Why do you look so upset? Introduce me, please."

Ganya, utterly disconcerted, introduced her first to Varya, and the two women exchanged strange looks before holding out their hands to each other. Nastasya Filippovna, however, laughed and masked her feelings with a show of good-humor; but Varya did not care to mask hers, and looked at her with gloomy intensity. Her countenance showed no trace even of the smile required by simple politeness. Ganya was aghast; it was useless to entreat, and there was no time indeed, and he flung at Varya such a menacing glance that she saw from it what the moment meant to her brother. She seemed to make up her mind to give in to him, and faintly smiled at Nastasya Filippovna. (All of the family were still very fond of one another.) The position was somewhat improved by Nina Alexandrovna, whom Ganya, helplessly confused, introduced after his sister. He even made the introduction to Nastasya Filippovna instead of to his mother. But no sooner had Nina Alexandrovna begun to speak of the "great pleasure," etc., when Nastasya Filippovna, paying no attention to her, turned hurriedly to Ganya and sitting down without waiting to be asked, on a little sofa in the corner by the window, she cried out:

"Where's your study? and . . . where are the lodgers? You take lodgers, don't you?"

Ganya flushed horribly and was stammering some answer, but Nastasya Filippovna added at once:

"Wherever do you keep lodgers here? You've no study

even. Does it pay?'' she asked, suddenly addressing Nina Alexandrovna.

"It's rather troublesome," the latter replied. "Of course it must pay to some extent, but we've only just . . .''

But Nastasya Filippovna was not listening again: she stared at Ganya, laughed, and shouted to him:

"What a face you make! My goodness! what a face — at this minute!''

Her laughter lasted several minutes, and Ganya's face certainly was terribly distorted. His stupefaction, his comic crestfallen confusion had suddenly left him. But he turned fearfully pale, his lips worked convulsively. He bent a silent, intent, and evil look on the face of his visitor, who still went on laughing.

There was another observer who had scarcely recovered from his amazement at the sight of Nastasya Filippovna; but though he stood dumbfounded in the same place by the drawing-room door, yet he noticed Ganya's pallor and the ominous change in his face. That observer was Myshkin. Almost frightened, he instinctively stepped forward.

"Drink some water,'' he murmured to Ganya, "and don't look like that.''

It was evident that he spoke on the impulse of the moment, without ulterior motive or intention. But his words produced an extraordinary effect. All Ganya's spite seemed suddenly turned against him. He seized him by the shoulder and looked at him in silence with hatred and resentment, as though unable to utter a word. It caused a general commotion; Nina Alexandrovna even uttered a faint cry. Ptitsyn stepped forward uneasily; Kolya and Ferdyshtchenko, who were coming in at the door, stopped short in amazement. Only Varya still looked sullen, yet she was watching intently. She did not sit down, but stood beside her mother with her arms folded across her bosom.

But Ganya checked himself at once, almost at the first moment, and laughed nervously. He regained his self-possession completely.

"Why, are you a doctor, prince?" he cried as simply and good-humoredly as he could. "He positively frightened me. Nastasya Filippovna, may I present? This is a rare personality, though I've only known him since the morning."

Nastasya Filippovna looked at Myshkin in astonishment.

"Prince? He is a prince? Only fancy, I took him for the footman just now and sent him in to announce me! Ha, ha, ha!"

"No harm done — no harm done," put in Ferdyshtchenko, going up to her quickly, relieved that they had begun to laugh. "No harm: if it's not true . . ."

"And I was almost swearing at you, prince! Forgive me, please. Ferdyshtchenko, how do you come to be here at such an hour? I did not expect to meet you here, anyway. Who? What prince? Myshkin?" she questioned Ganya, who, still holding Myshkin by the shoulder, had by now introduced him.

"Our boarder," repeated Ganya.

It was obvious that they presented him and almost thrust him upon Nastasya Filippovna as a curiosity, as a means of escape from a false position. Myshkin distinctly caught the word "idiot" pronounced behind his back, probably by Ferdyshtchenko, as though in explanation to Nastasya Filippovna.

"Tell me, why didn't you undeceive me just now when I made such a dreadful mistake about you?" Nastasya Filippovna went on, scanning Myshkin from head to foot in a most unceremonious fashion.

She waited with impatience for an answer, as though she were sure the answer would be so stupid as to make them laugh.

"I was surprised at seeing you so suddenly," Myshkin muttered.

"And how did you know it was I? Where have you seen me before? But how is it? Really, it seems as though I had seen him somewhere. And tell me why were you so astonished just now? What is there so amazing about me?"

"Come now, come," Ferdyshtchenko went on, simpering. "Come now! Oh Lord, the things I'd say in answer to such a question! Come! . . . We shall think you are a duffer next, prince!"

"I should say them too in your place," said Myshkin, laughing, to Ferdyshtchenko. "I was very much struck to-day by your portrait," he went on, addressing Nastasya Filippovna. "Then I talked to the Epanchins about you; and early this morning in the train, before I reached Petersburg, Parfyon Rogozhin told me a great deal about you . . . And at the very minute I opened the door to you, I was thinking about you too, and then suddenly you appeared."

"And how did you recognize that it was I?"

"From the photograph, and . . ."

"And what?"

"And you were just as I had imagined you . . . I feel as though I had seen you somewhere too."

"Where — where?"

"I feel as though I had seen your eyes somewhere . . . but that's impossible. That's nonsense . . . I've never been here before. Perhaps in a dream . . ."

"Bravo, prince!" cried Ferdyshtchenko. "Yes, I take back my 'if it's not true.' But it's all his innocence," he added regretfully.

Myshkin had uttered his few sentences in an uneasy

voice, often stopping to take breath. Everything about him suggested strong emotion. Nastasya Filippovna looked at him with interest, but she was not laughing now.

Suddenly there was a great deal of noise and many people in the entry. From the drawing-room it sounded as though several people had already come in and more were still coming. Several voices were talking and shouting at once. There was shouting and talking on the staircase also; the door opening on it had evidently not been closed. The visit seemed to be a very strange one. They all looked at each other. Ganya rushed into the dining room, but several visitors had already entered it.

"Ah, here he is, the Judas!" cried a voice that Myshkin knew. "How are you, Ganya, you scoundrel?"

"Here he is, here he is himself," another voice chimed in.

Myshkin could not be mistaken: the first voice was Rogozhin's, the second Lebedyev's.

Ganya stood petrified and gazing at them in silence in the doorway from the drawing room, not hindering ten or twelve persons from following Parfyon Rogozhin into the dining room. The party was an exceedingly mixed one, and not only diverse but disorderly. Some of them walked in as they were, in their overcoats and furs. None was quite drunk, however, though they all seemed extremely exhilarated. They seemed to need each other's moral support to enter; not one would have had the effrontery to enter alone, but they all seemed to push one another in. Even Rogozhin walked diffidently at the head of the party; but he had some intention, and he seemed in a state of gloomy and irritated preoccupation. The others only made a chorus or band of supporters. Besides Lebedyev, there was Zalyozhev, who had flung off his overcoat in the entry and walked in swaggering and jaunty with his hair curled. There were two or three more of the same sort, evidently young merchants; a man in a semi-military greatcoat; a very fat little man who kept laughing continually; an immense man over six feet, also very stout, extremely taciturn and morose, who evidently put his faith in his fists. There was a medical student, and a little Pole who had somehow attached himself to the party. Two nondescript ladies peeped in at the front door, but did not venture to come in. Kolya slammed the door in their faces and latched it.

"How are you, Ganya, you scoundrel? You didn't expect Parfyon Rogozhin, did you?" repeated Rogozhin, going to the drawing room door and facing Ganya.

But at that moment he caught sight of Nastasya Filippovna, who sat facing him in the drawing room. Evidently nothing was further from his thoughts than meeting her here, for the sight of her had an extraordinary effect on him. He turned so pale that his lips went blue.

"Then it's true," he said quietly, as though to himself, looking absolutely distracted. "It's the end! . . . Well . . . you shall pay for it!" he snarled, suddenly looking with extreme fury at Ganya. "Well . . . curses!"

He gasped for breath, he could hardly speak. Mechanically he moved into the drawing room, but as he went in, he suddenly saw Nina Alexandrovna and Varya and stopped, somewhat embarrassed, in spite of his emotion. After him came Lebedyev, who followed him about like a shadow and was very drunk; then the student, the gentleman with the fists, Zalyozhev, bowing to right and left, and last of all the little fat man squeezed himself in. The presence of the ladies was still a check on them, and it was evidently an unwelcome constraint, which would of course have broken down if they had once been set off, if some pretext for shouting and beginning a row had arisen. Then all the ladies in the world would not have hindered them.

"What, you here too, prince?" Rogozhin said absently,

somewhat surprised at meeting Myshkin. "Still in your gaiters, huh?" he sighed, forgetting Myshkin's existence and looking towards Nastasya Filippovna again, moving closer to her as though drawn by a magnet.

Nastasya Filippovna too looked with uneasy curiosity at the visitors.

Ganya recovered himself at last.

"But allow me. What does this mean?" he began in a loud voice, looking severely at the newcomers and addressing himself principally to Rogozhin. "This isn't a stable, gentlemen, my mother and sister are here."

"We see your mother and sister are here," muttered Rogozhin through his teeth.

"That can be seen, that your mother and sister are here." Lebedyev felt called upon to second the statement.

The gentleman with the fists, feeling no doubt that the moment had arrived, began growling something.

"But upon my word!" cried Ganya, suddenly exploding and raising his voice immoderately. "First, I beg you all to go into the dining room, and secondly, kindly let me know . . ."

"Fancy, he doesn't know me!" said Rogozhin, with an angry grin, not budging from where he stood. "Don't you know Rogozhin?"

"I've certainly met you somewhere, but . . ."

"Met me somewhere! Why, I lost two hundred rubles of my father's money to you three months ago. The old man died without finding it out. You enticed me into it and Kniff cheated. Don't you recognize me? Ptitsyn was a witness of it. If I were to show you three rubles out of my pocket, you'd crawl on all fours to Vassilyevsky for it — that's the sort of chap you are! That's the sort of soul you've got! And I've come here now to buy you out for cash. Never mind my having come with such boots on. I've got a mint of money now, brother, I can buy the whole of you and your live-stock

too. I can buy you all up, if I like! I'll buy up everything!''
Rogozhin grew more and more excited and seemed more and
more drunk. "To hell with it!" he cried. "Nastasya Filipp-
povna, don't turn me away. Tell me one thing: are you going
to marry him, or not?''

Rogozhin put this question desperately, as though
appealing to a deity, but with the courage of a man condemned to death who has nothing to lose. In deadly anguish
he awaited her reply.

With haughty and sarcastic eyes, Nastasya Filippovna
looked him up and down. But she glanced at Varya and Nina
Alexandrovna, looked at Ganya, and suddenly changed her
tone.

"Certainly not! What's the matter with you? And what
has put it into your head to ask such a question?'' she
answered quietly and gravely and as it seemed with some
surprise.

"No? No!" cried Rogozhin, almost frantic with delight.
"Then you are not? But they told me . . . Ach! . . . Nastasya
Filippovna, they say that you are engaged to Ganya. To him!
As though that were possible! I told them all it was impossible. I can buy him up for a hundred rubles. If I were to give
him a thousand, three thousand, to withdraw, he would run
off on his wedding day and leave his bride to me. That's right,
isn't it, Ganya, you scoundrel? You'd take the three thousand, wouldn't you? Here's the money — here you have it! I
came to get you to sign the agreement to do it. I said I'll buy
him off and I will buy him off!''

"Get out of the room, you are drunk!" cried Ganya,
who had been flushing and growing pale by turns.

His outburst was followed by a sudden explosion from
several persons at once: the whole crew of Rogozhin's fol-
lowers were only awaiting the signal for battle. With intense

solitude Lebedyev was whispering something in Rogozhin's ear.

"You're right, clerk!" answered Rogozhin. "Right, you drunken soul! Well, here goes! Nastasya Filippovna," he cried, gazing at her like a maniac, passing from timidity to the extreme of audacity, "here are eighteen thousand rubles!" and he tossed on the table before her a roll of notes wrapped in white paper and tied with string. "There! And . . . and there's more to come!"

He did not venture to say what he wanted.

"No, no, no!" Lebedyev whispered to him with an air of dismay.

It could be guessed that he was horrified at the magnitude of the sum and was urging him to try his luck with a much smaller one.

"No, brother, you are a fool; you don't know how to behave here . . . and it seems as though I am a fool like you!" Rogozhin started, and checked himself as he met the flashing eyes of Nastasya Filippovna. "Aah! I've made a mess of it, listening to you," he added with intense regret.

Nastasya Filippovna suddenly laughed as she looked at Rogozhin's downcast face.

"Eighteen thousand to me? Ah, one can see the peasant he is!" she added with insolent familiarity, and she got up from the sofa, as though to go away.

Ganya had watched the whole scene with a sinking heart.

"Forty thousand, then — forty, not eighteen!" cried Rogozhin. "Ptitsyn and Biskup promised to get me forty thousand by seven o'clock. Forty thousand! Cash down!"

The scene had become scandalous in the extreme, but Nastasya Filippovna stayed on and still went on laughing, as though she were intentionally prolonging it. Nina Alexandrovna and Varya had also risen from their places and waited in silent dismay to see how much further it would go. Varya's eyes glittered, but the effect of it all on Nina Alexandrovna was painful; she trembled and seemed on the point of fainting.

"A hundred, then, if that's it! I'll give you a hundred thousand to-day. Ptitsyn, lend it me, it'll be worth your while!"

"You are mad," Ptitsyn whispered suddenly, going up to him quickly and taking him by the hand. "You are mad! They'll send for the police! Where are you?"

"He is drunk and boasting," said Nastasya Filippovna, as though taunting him.

"I am not boasting, I'll get the money before evening. Ptitsyn, lend it to me, you loan shark! Ask what you like for it. Get me a hundred thousand this evening! I'll show that I won't stop at anything." Rogozhin was in an ecstasy of excitement . . .

"Is there no one among you who will take this shameless woman away?" exclaimed Varya, quivering all over with anger.

"They call me a shameless woman," Nastasya Filippovna answered back with contemptuous gaiety. "And I came like a fool to invite them to my party this evening. That's how your sister treats me, Gavril Ardalionovitch!"

For some time Ganya stood as though thunderstruck at his sister's outburst, but seeing that Nastasya Filippovna really was going this time, he rushed frantically at Varya and seized her arm in a fury.

"What have you done?" he cried, looking at her, as though he would have withered her on the spot.

He was utterly beside himself and hardly knew what he was doing.

"What have I done? Where are you dragging me? Is it to

beg her pardon for having insulted your mother and for having come here to disgrace your family, you base creature?" Varya cried again, looking with triumphant defiance at her brother.

For an instant they stood so, facing one another. Ganya still kept hold of her arm. Twice Varya tried with all her might to pull herself free but suddenly losing all self-control, she spat in her brother's face.

"What a girl!" cried Nastasya Filippovna. "Bravo! Ptitsyn, I congratulate you!"

Everything danced before Ganya's eyes, and completely forgetting himself, he struck at his sister with all his might. He would have hit her on the face, but suddenly another hand caught Ganya's. Myshkin stood between him and his sister.

"Don't, that's enough," he brought out insistently, though he was shaking all over with violent emotion.

"Blast it! Are you always going to get in my way?" roared Ganya. He let go Varya's arm and, mad with rage, gave Myshkin a violent slap in the face with the hand thus freed.

"Ah!" cried Kolya, clasping his hands. "My God!"

Exclamations were heard on all sides. Myshkin turned pale. He looked Ganya straight in the face with strange and reproachful eyes; his lips quivered, trying to articulate something; they were twisted into a sort of strange and utterly incongruous smile.

"Well, you may strike me . . . but her . . . I won't let you," he said softly at last.

But suddenly he broke down, left Ganya, hid his face in his hands, moved away to a corner of the room, stood with his face to the wall, and in a breaking voice said:

"Oh, how ashamed you will be of what you've done!"

Ganya did, indeed, stand looking utterly crushed. Kolya rushed to hug and kiss Myshkin. He was followed by

Rogozhin, Varya, Ptitsyn, Nina Alexandrovna — all the party, even the general, who all crowded about Myshkin.

"Never mind, never mind," muttered Myshkin in all directions, still with the same incongruous smile.

"And he will regret it," cried Rogozhin. "You will be ashamed, Ganya, that you have insulted such a . . . sheep" (he could not find another word). "Prince darling, drop them; curse them and come along. I'll show you what a friend Rogozhin can be."

Nastasya Filippovna too was very much impressed by Ganya's action and Myshkin's answer. Her usually pale and pensive face, which had seemed all along so out of keeping with her affected laughter, was evidently stirred by a new feeling. Yet she still seemed unwilling to betray it and to be trying to maintain a certain sarcastic expression.

"I certainly have seen his face somewhere," she said, speaking quite earnestly now, suddenly recalling her former question.

"Aren't you ashamed? Surely you are not what you are pretending to be now? It isn't possible!" cried Myshkin suddenly with deep and heartfelt reproach.

Nastasya Filippovna was surprised and smiled, seeming to hide something under her smile. She looked at Ganya, rather confused, and walked out of the drawing room. But before reaching the entry, she turned sharply, went quickly up to Nina Alexandrovna, took her hand and raised it to her lips.

"I really am not like this, he is right," she said in a rapid eager whisper, flushing hotly; and turning around, she walked out so quickly that no one had time to realise what she had come back for.

The Awakening of Lazarus

Raskolnikov, the main character of the novel Crime and Punishment, *has murdered both an old woman who is a money-lender and a youthful relative of hers called Lizaveta, who had just happened to come in and who is mentioned several times. Raskolnikov committed the murder "to prove to himself that he was a man and not a louse." Now, right after the deed, his inner collapse begins. He admits that the act itself was wrong, even though he is still trying to persuade himself that it wouldn't have been wrong if only he had measured up to it. He intends to turn himself in and has basically done so already through careless remarks. But first he wants to assure himself of at least one sympathetic and forgiving soul, since he cannot bear the loneliness caused by his unconfessed deed.*

Sonia Marmeladov, whom he then visits, had become a prostitute so as to be able to help her tubercular stepmother Katerina Ivanovna and Katerina's sick children. (All women's work in those days received extremely low pay.) Her father, formerly a minor official and also an incurable drunkard, had been run over and killed just the day before. Raskolnikov had once met this man in a low-class tavern or bar and after hearing from him the whole story of his family had then taken him home. Right after Marmeladov's death he had given the widow all the money he had.

Raskolnikov went straight to the house on the canal bank where Sonia lived. It was an old green house of three stories. He found the porter and obtained from him vague directions as to the whereabouts of Kapernaumov, the tailor. Having found in the corner of the courtyard the entrance to the dark and narrow staircase, he mounted to the second floor and came out onto a gallery that ran round the whole second story over the yard. While he was wandering in the darkness, uncertain where to turn for Kapernaumov's door, a door opened three paces from him; he mechanically took hold of it.

"Who is there?" a woman's voice asked uneasily.

"It's I — come to see you," answered Raskolnikov, and he walked into the tiny entry.

On a broken chair stood a candle in a battered copper candlestick.

"It's you! Good heavens!" cried Sonia weakly, and she stood rooted to the spot.

"Which is your room? This way?" and Raskolnikov, trying not to look at her, hastened in.

A minute later Sonia too came in with the candle, put down the candlestick and, completely disconcerted, stood before him indescribably agitated and apparently frightened by his unexpected visit. The color rushed suddenly to her pale face and tears came into her eyes . . . She felt sick and ashamed and happy, too . . . Raskolnikov turned away quickly and sat on a chair by the table. He scanned the room in a glance.

It was a large but exceedingly low-pitched room, the only one let by the Kapernaumovs, whose rooms were beyond a closed door in the wall on the left. On the opposite side in the right-hand wall was another door, always kept locked. That led to the next flat, which formed a separate lodging. Sonia's room looked like a barn; it was a very irregular quadrangle and this gave it a grotesque appearance. A wall with three windows looking out onto the canal ran aslant so that one corner formed a very acute angle, and it was difficult to see in it without very strong light. The other corner was disproportionately obtuse. There was scarcely any furniture in the big room: in the corner on the right was a bedstead, beside it, nearest the door, a chair. A plain wooden table covered with a blue cloth stood against the same wall, close to the door into the other flat. Two rush-bottom chairs stood by the table. On the opposite wall near the acute angle stood a small plain wooden chest of drawers looking, as it were, lost in a desert. That was all there was in the room. The yellow, scratched, and shabby wallpaper was black in the corners. It must have been damp and full of coal fumes in the winter. There was every sign of poverty; even the bedstead had no curtain.

Sonia looked in silence at her visitor (who was so attentively and unceremoniously scrutinizing her room) and began at last to tremble with terror, as though she was standing before her judge and the arbiter of her destinies.

"I am late. . . . It's eleven, isn't it?" he asked, still not lifting his eyes.

"Yes," muttered Sonia, "Oh, yes, it is," she added hastily, as though in that lay her means of escape. "My landlady's clock has just struck . . . I heard it myself . . ."

"I've come to you for the last time," Raskolnikov went on gloomily, although this was the first time. "I may perhaps not see you again . . ."

"Are you . . . going away?"

"I don't know . . . to-morrow . . ."

"Then you are not coming to Katerina Ivanovna tomorrow?" Sonia's voice shook.

"I don't know. I shall know to-morrow morning . . . Never mind that: I've come to say one word . . ."

He raised his brooding eyes to her and suddenly noticed that he was sitting down while she was all the while standing before him.

"Why are you standing? Sit down," he said in a changed voice, gentle and friendly.

She sat down. He looked kindly and almost compassionately at her.

"How thin you are! What a hand! Quite transparent, like a dead hand."

He took her hand. Sonia smiled faintly.

"I have always been like that," she said.

"Even when you lived at home?"

"Yes."

"Of course you were," he added abruptly and the expression of his face and the sound of his voice changed again suddenly. He looked round him once more.

"You rent this room from the Kapernaumovs?"

"Yes . . ."

"They live there, through that door?"

"Yes . . . They have another room like this."

"All in one room?"

"Yes."

"I should be afraid in your room at night," he observed gloomily.

"They are very good people, very kind," answered Sonia, who still seemed bewildered, "and all the furniture, everything . . . everything is theirs. And they are very kind, and the children, too, often come to see me."

"They all stammer, don't they?"

"Yes . . . He stammers and he's lame. And his wife too . . . it's not exactly that she stammers, but she can't speak plainly. She is a very kind woman. And he used to be a house serf. And there are seven children . . . and it's only the eldest one that stammers and the others are simply ill . . . but they don't stammer . . . But where did you hear about them?'' she added with some surprise.

"Your father told me. He told me all about you . . . And how you went out at six o'clock and came back at nine and how Katerina Ivanovna knelt down by your bed."

Sonia was confused.

"I fancied I saw him to-day," she whispered hesitatingly.

"Whom?"

"Father. I was walking out there at the corner about ten o'clock, and he seemed to be walking in front. It looked just like him. I wanted to go to Katerina Ivanovna . . ."

"You were walking in the streets?"

"Yes," Sonia whispered abruptly, again overcome with confusion and looking down.

"Katerina Ivanovna used to beat you, I daresay?"

"Oh no, what are you saying? No!" Sonia looked at him almost with dismay.

"You love her, then?"

"Love her? Of course!" said Sonia with plaintive emphasis, and she clasped her hands in distress. "Ah, you don't . . . If you only knew! You see, she is quite like a child . . . Her mind is quite unhinged, you see . . . from sorrow. And how clever she used to be . . . how generous . . . how kind! Ah, you don't understand, you don't understand!"

Sonia said this as though in despair, wringing her hands in excitement and distress. Her pale cheeks flushed, there was a look of anguish in her eyes. It was clear that she was stirred to the very depths, that she was longing to speak, to implore, to express something. A sort of *insatiable* compassion, if one may so express it, was reflected in every feature of her face.

"Beat me! How can you? Good heavens, beat me! And if she did beat me, what then? What of it? You know nothing, nothing about it . . . She is so unhappy . . . ah, how unhappy!

And ill . . . She is seeking righteousness, she is pure. She has such faith that there must be righteousness everywhere and she expects it . . . And if you were to torture her, she wouldn't do wrong. She doesn't see that it's impossible for people to be righteous, and she is angry at it. Like a child, like a child! She is good!"

"And what will happen to you?"

Sonia looked at him inquiringly.

"They are left on your hands, you see. They were all on your hands before, though . . . And your father came to you to beg for drink. Well, how will it be now?"

"I don't know," Sonia articulated mournfully.

"Will they stay there?"

"I don't know . . . They are in debt for the lodging, but the landlady, I hear, said to-day that she wanted to get rid of them, and Katerina Ivanovna says that she won't stay another minute."

"How is it she is so bold? She relies upon you?"

"Oh no, don't talk like that . . . We are one, we live like one." Sonia was agitated again and even angry, as though a canary or some other little bird were to be angry. "And what could she do? What, what could she do?" she persisted, getting hot and excited. "And how she cried to-day! Her mind is unhinged, haven't you noticed it? At one minute she is worrying like a child that everything should be right tomorrow, the lunch and all that . . . Then she is wringing her hands, spitting blood, weeping, and all at once she will begin knocking her head against the wall in despair. Then she will be comforted again. She builds all her hopes on you; she says that you will help her now and that she will borrow a little money somewhere and go to her native town with me and set up a boarding school for the daughters of gentlemen and take me to superintend it, and we will begin a new splendid life. And she kisses and hugs me, comforts me, and you know she has such faith, such faith in her dreams! One can't contradict her. And all the day long she has been washing, cleaning, mending. She dragged the washtub into the room with her feeble hands and sank on the bed, gasping for breath. We went to the shops this morning to buy shoes for Polenka and Lida, for theirs are quite worn out. Only the money we'd reckoned wasn't enough, not nearly enough. And she picked out such dear little boots, for she has taste, you just don't know. And there in the shop she burst out crying before the shopmen because she hadn't enough . . . Ah, it was sad to see her . . ."

"Well, after that I can understand that you are living the way you are," Raskolnikov said with a bitter smile.

"And aren't you sorry for them? Aren't you sorry?" Sonia flew at him again. "Why, I know you gave your last penny yourself though you'd seen nothing of it, and if you'd seen everything, oh dear! And how often, how often I've brought her to tears! Only last week! Yes, I! Only a week before his death. I was cruel! And how often I've done it! Ah, I've been wretched at the thought of it all day!"

Sonia wrung her hands as she spoke at the pain of remembering it.

"You were cruel?"

"Yes, I — I! I went to see them," she went on, weeping, "and father said, 'Read me something, my head aches, read to me . . . here's a book.' He had a book he had got from Andrey Semyonovitch Lebeziatnikov — he lives there — he always used to get hold of such queer books. And I said, 'I can't stay,' as I didn't want to read, and I'd gone in chiefly to show Katerina Ivanovna my lace collars. Lizaveta, the pedlar, sold me some collars and cuffs cheap — pretty, new, embroidered ones. Katerina Ivanovna liked them very much; she put them on and looked at herself in the glass and was delighted with them. 'Make me a present of them, Sonia,' she said, 'please do. *Please do!'* She wanted them so much. And when could she wear them? They just reminded her of her old happy days. She looked at herself in the glass, admired herself, and she has no nice clothes at all, nothing like that of her own, hasn't had all these years! And she never asks anyone for anything; she is proud, she'd sooner give away everything. And these she asked for, she liked them so much. And I didn't want to give them. 'What use are they to you, Katerina Ivanovna?' I said. I spoke like that to her; I ought not to have said that! She gave me such a look. And she was so grieved, so grieved at my refusing her. And it was so sad to see . . . And she was not grieved for the collars but for my refusing, I saw that. Ah, if only I could bring it all back, change it, take back those words! Ah, if I . . . but it's nothing to you!''

"Did you know Lizaveta, the pedlar?"

"Yes . . . Did you know her?" Sonia asked with some surprise.

"Katerina Ivanovna has consumption, rapid consumption; she will soon die," said Raskolnikov after a pause, without answering her question.

"Oh, no, no, no!"

And Sonia unconsciously clutched both his hands, as though imploring that she should not die.

"But it will be better if she dies."

"No, not better, not at all better!" Sonia unconsciously repeated, frightened, and not considering her words.

"And the children? What can you do except take them to live with you?"

"Oh, I don't know," cried Sonia, almost in despair, and she put her hands to her head.

It was evident that that idea had very often occurred to her before, and he had only roused it again.

"And what if even now, while Katerina Ivanovna is

alive, you get ill and are taken to the hospital, what will happen then?'' he persisted pitilessly.

"How can you? That cannot be!''

And Sonia's face worked with awful terror.

"Cannot be?'' Raskolnikov went on with a harsh smile. "You are not insured, are you? What will happen to them then? They will be in the street, all of them, she will cough and beg and knock her head against some wall as she did today, and the children will cry . . . Then she will fall down, be taken to the police station and to the hospital, she will die, and the children . . .''

"Oh, no . . . God will not let that happen!'' broke at last from Sonia's anguished heart.

She listened, looking imploringly at him, clasping her hands in dumb entreaty, as though it all depended upon him.

Raskolnikov got up and began to walk about the room. A minute passed. Sonia was standing with her hands and her head hanging in terrible dejection.

"And can't you save? Put by for a rainy day?'' he asked, stopping suddenly before her.

"No,'' whispered Sonia.

"Of course not. Have you tried?'' he added almost ironically.

"Yes.''

"And it didn't come off! Of course not! No need to ask.''

And again he paced the room. Another minute passed.

"You don't get money every day?''

Sonia was more embarrassed than ever, and color rushed into her face again.

"No,'' she whispered with a painful effort.

"It will be the same with Polenka, no doubt,'' he said suddenly.

"No, no! It can't be, no!" Sonia cried aloud in desperation, as though she had been stabbed. "God would not allow anything so awful!"

"He lets others come to it."

"No, no! God will protect her — God!" she repeated beside herself.

"But, perhaps there is no God at all," Raskolnikov answered with obvious malice, laughed, and looked at her.

Sonia's face suddenly changed; a tremor passed over it. She looked at him with unutterable reproach, tried to say something, but could not speak and broke into bitter, bitter sobs, hiding her face in her hands.

"You say Katerina Ivanovna's mind is unhinged; your own mind is unhinged," he said after a brief silence.

Five minutes passed. He still paced up and down the room in silence, not looking at her. At last he went up to her; his eyes glittered. He put his two hands on her shoulders and looked straight into her tearful face. His eyes were hard, feverish, and piercing; his lips were twitching. All at once he bent down quickly and, dropping to the ground, kissed her foot. Sonia drew back from him as from a madman. And certainly he looked like a madman.

"What are you doing to me?" she muttered, turning pale, and a sudden anguish clutched at her heart.

He stood up at once.

"I did not bow down to you, I bowed down to all the suffering of humanity," he said wildly and walked away to the window. "Listen," he added, turning to her a minute later. "I said just now to an insolent man that he was not worth your little finger . . . and that I did my sister honor by seating her beside you."

"Ach, you said that to them? And in her presence?" cried Sonia frightened. "Sit down with me! An honor! Why, I'm . . . dishonorable . . . Ah, why did you say that?"

"It was not because of your dishonor and your sin I said that of you, but because of your great suffering. But you are a great sinner, that's true," he added almost solemnly, "and your worst sin is that you have destroyed and betrayed yourself *for nothing*. Isn't that fearful? Isn't it fearful that you are living in this filth that you loathe so, and at the same time you know yourself (you've only to open your eyes) that you are not helping anyone or saving anyone from anything! Tell me," he went on almost in a frenzy, "how this shame and degradation can exist in you side by side with other, opposite, holy feelings? It would be better, a thousand times better and wiser, to leap into the water and end it all!"

"But what would become of them?" Sonia asked faintly, gazing at him with eyes of anguish, but not seeming surprised at his suggestion.

Raskolnikov looked strangely at her. He read it all in her face; so she must have had that thought already, perhaps many times, and in her despair had thought out in detail how to end it and so earnestly that now she scarcely wondered at his suggestion. She had not even noticed the cruelty of his words. (The significance of his reproaches and his peculiar attitude to her shame she had, of course, not noticed either, and that too was clear to him.) But he saw how monstrously the thought of her disgraceful, shameful position was torturing her and had long tortured her. "What, what," he thought, "could hitherto have hindered her from putting an end to it?" Only then he realized what those poor little orphan children and that pitiful half-crazy Katerina Ivanovna, knocking her head against the wall in her consumption, meant to Sonia.

Nevertheless, it was clear to him again that considering her character and the amount of education she had after all received, she could not stay as she was in any case. He was still confronted by the question how could she have remained so long in that position without going out of her mind, since she could not bring herself to jump into the water? Of course he knew that Sonia's lot was an unusual one, though unhappily not unique. Yet that very exceptional nature of her previous life with a tinge of education might, one would have thought, have killed her at the first step on that revolting path. What held her up — surely not depravity? All that infamy had obviously only touched her mechanically, not one drop of real depravity had penetrated to her heart; he saw that. He saw through her as she stood before him . . .

"There are three choices before her," he thought, "the canal, the madhouse, or . . . at last to sink into the depravity that obscures the mind and turns the heart to stone."

The last idea was the most revolting, but he was a sceptic, he was young, abstract, and therefore cruel, and so he could not help believing that the last end was the most likely.

"But can that be true?" he cried to himself. "Can that creature who has still preserved the purity of her spirit be consciously drawn at last into that sink of filth and iniquity? Can the process already have begun? Can it be that she has only been able to bear it till now because vice has begun to be less loathsome to her? No, no, that cannot be!" he cried, as Sonia had just before. "No, what has kept her from the canal till now is the idea of sin . . . and they, the children . . . And if she has not gone out of her mind . . . but who says she has not gone out of her mind? Is she in her senses? Can one talk, can one reason as she does? How can she sit on the edge of the abyss of loathsomeness into which she is slipping and refuse to listen when she is told of danger? Does she expect a miracle? No doubt she does. Doesn't that all mean madness?"

He stayed obstinately at that thought. He liked that explanation, indeed better than any other. He began looking more intently at her.

"So you pray to God a great deal, Sonia?" he asked her.

Sonia did not speak; he stood beside her waiting for an answer.

"What should I be without God?" she whispered rapidly, forcefully, glancing at him with suddenly flashing eyes, squeezing his hand.

"Ah, so that is it!" he thought.

"And what does God do for you?" he asked, probing her further.

Sonia was silent a long while, as though she could not answer. Her weak chest kept heaving with emotion.

"Be silent! Don't ask! You are unworthy!" she cried suddenly, looking sternly and wrathfully at him.

"That's it, that's it," he repeated to himself.

"He does everything," she whispered quickly, looking down again.

"That's the way out! That's the explanation," he decided, scrutinizing her with eager curiosity, with a new, strange, almost morbid feeling. He gazed at that pale, thin, irregular, angular little face, those soft blue eyes, which could flash with such fire, such stern energy, that little body still shaking with indignation and anger — and it all seemed to him more and more strange, almost impossible. "She is a religious maniac!" he repeated to himself.

There was a book lying on the chest of drawers. He had noticed it every time he paced up and down the room. Now he took it up and looked at it. It was the New Testament in the Russian translation. It was bound in leather, old and worn.

"Where did you get that?" he called to her across the room.

She was still standing in the same place, three steps from the table.

"It was brought me," she answered, as it were unwillingly, not looking at him.

"Who brought it?"

"Lizaveta. I asked her for it."

"Lizaveta! Strange!" he thought.

Everything about Sonia seemed to him stranger and more wonderful every moment. He carried the book to the candle and began to turn over the pages.

"Where is the story of Lazarus?" he asked suddenly.

Sonia looked obstinately at the ground and would not answer. She was standing sideways to the table.

"Where is the raising of Lazarus? Find it for me, Sonia."

She stole a glance at him.

"You are not looking in the right place . . . It's in the fourth gospel," she whispered sternly, without looking at him.

"Find it and read it to me," he said. He sat down with his elbow on the table, leaned his head on his hand and looked away sullenly, prepared to listen.

"In three weeks' time they'll welcome her in the madhouse! I shall be there too if I am not in a worse place," he muttered to himself.

Sonia heard Raskolnikov's request distrustfully and moved hesitatingly to the table. She took the book, however.

"Haven't you read it?" she asked, looking up at him across the table.

Her voice became sterner and sterner.

"Long ago . . . When I was at school. Read!"

"And haven't you heard it in church?"

"I . . . haven't been. Do you often go?"

"N-no," whispered Sonia.

Raskolnikov smiles. "I understand . . . And you won't go to your father's funeral tomorrow?"

"Yes, I shall. I was at church last week, too . . . I had a requiem service."

"For whom?"

"For Lizaveta. She was killed with an axe."

His nerves were more and more strained. His head began to go round.

"Were you friends with Lizaveta?"

"Yes . . . She was good . . . she used to come . . . not often . . . she couldn't . . . We used to read together and . . . talk. She will see God."

The last phrase sounded strange in his ears. And here was something new again: the mysterious meetings with Lizaveta — and both of them religious maniacs.

"I shall be a religious maniac myself soon! It's infectious. Read!" he cried irritably and insistently.

Sonia still hesitated. Her heart was throbbing. She hardly dared to read to him. He looked almost with exasperation at the "unhappy lunatic."

"What for? You don't believe? . . ." she whispered softly and as it were breathlessly.

"Read! I want you to," he persisted. "You used to read to Lizaveta."

Sonia opened the book and found the place. Her hands were shaking, her voice failed her. Twice she tried to begin and could not bring out the first syllable.

"Now a certain man was sick named Lazarus of Bethany . . ." she forced herself at last to read, but at the third word her voice broke like an overstrained string. There was a catch in her breath.

Raskolnikov saw in part why Sonia could not bring herself to read to him and the more he saw this, the more roughly and irritably he insisted on her doing so. He understood only too well how painful it was for her to betray and unveil all that was her *own*. He understood that these feelings really were her *secret treasure*, which she had kept perhaps for years, perhaps from childhood, while she lived with an unhappy father and a distracted stepmother crazed by grief, in the midst of starving children and unseemly abuse and reproaches. But at the same time he knew now and knew for certain that, although it filled her with dread and suffering, yet she had a tormenting desire to read and to read to *him* that he might hear it, and to read *now* — whatever might come of it! . . . He read this in her eyes, he could see it in her intense emotion. She mastered herself, controlled the spasm in her throat, and went on reading the eleventh chapter of St. John and came to the nineteenth verse:

"And many of the Jews came to Martha and Mary, to comfort them concerning their brother."

"Then Martha, as soon as she heard that Jesus was coming, went and met him; but Mary sat still in the house.

"Then said Martha unto Jesus, Lord, if thou hadst been here, my brother had not died.

"But I know, that even now, whatsoever thou wilt ask of God, God will give it thee . . ."

Then she stopped again with a shamefaced feeling that her voice would quiver and break again.

"Jesus said unto her, thy brother shall rise again.

"Martha saith unto him, I know that he shall rise again in the resurrection at the last day.

"Jesus said unto her, I am the resurrection, and the life: he that believeth in me, though he were dead, yet shall he live:

"And whosoever liveth and believeth in me shall never die. Believest thou this?

"She saith unto him," — and drawing a painful breath, Sonia read distinctly and forcibly as though she were making a public confession of faith — "Yea, Lord: I believe that thou art the Christ, the Son of God, which should come into the world."

She stopped and looked up quickly at him, but controlling herself went on reading. Raskolnikov sat without moving, his elbows on the table and his eyes turned away. She read on to the thirty-second verse.

"Then when Mary was come where Jesus was, and saw him, she fell down at his feet, saying unto him, Lord, if thou hadst been here, my brother had not died.

"When Jesus therefore saw her weeping, and the Jews also weeping which came with her, he groaned in the spirit, and was troubled, and said, Where have ye laid him? They said unto him, Lord, come and see.

"Jesus wept.

"Then said the Jews, Behold how he loved him!

"And some of them said, Could not this Man, which opened the eyes of the blind, have caused that even this man should not have died?"

Raskolnikov turned and looked at her with emotion. Yes, he had known it! She was trembling in a real physical fever. He had expected it. She was getting near the story of the greatest miracle, and a feeling of immense triumph came over her. Her voice rang out like a bell; triumph and joy gave it power. The lines danced before her eyes, but she knew what she was reading by heart. Dropping her voice at the last verse, "Could not this Man which opened the eyes of the blind, . . ." she passionately reproduced the doubt, the reproach, and censure of the blind, disbelieving Jews, who in another moment would fall at His feet as though struck by thunder, sobbing and believing . . . "And *he, he too*, who is blinded and unbelieving, he too will hear, he too will believe. Yes, yes! At once, now!" was what she was dreaming, and she was quivering with happy anticipation.

"Jesus therefore again groaning in himself cometh to the grave. It was a cave, and a stone lay upon it.

"Jesus said, Take ye away the stone. Martha, the sister of him that was dead, saith unto Him, Lord, by this time he stinketh: for he hath been dead *four* days."

She laid emphasis on the word four.

"Jesus saith unto her, Said I not unto thee, that, if thou wouldest believe, thou shouldst see the glory of God?

"Then they took away the stone from the place where the dead was laid. And Jesus lifted up his eyes, and said, Father, I thank thee that thou hast heard me. And I knew that thou hearest me always: but because of the people which stand by I said it, that they may believe that thou hast sent me.

"And when he thus had spoken, he cried with a loud voice, Lazarus, come forth.

"And he that was dead came forth," (she read loudly, cold and trembling with ecstasy, as though she were seeing it before her eyes) "bound hand and foot with graveclothes: and his face was bound about with a napkin. Jesus saith unto them, Loose him, and let him go.

"Then many of the Jews which came to Mary, and had seen the things which Jesus did, believed on him."

She could read no more, closed the book and got up from her chair quickly.

"That is all about the raising of Lazarus," she whispered severely and abruptly, and turning away she stood motionless, not daring to raise her eyes to him. She still trembled feverishly. The candle-end was flickering out in the battered candlestick, dimly lighting up the poverty-stricken room and the murderer and the harlot, who had so strangely been reading together the eternal book. Five minutes or more passed.

"I came to speak of something," Raskolnikov said aloud, frowning. He got up and went to Sonia. She lifted her eyes to him in silence. His face was particularly stern, and there was a sort of savage determination in it.

"I have abandoned my family today," he said, "my mother and sister. I am not going to see them. I've broken with them completely."

"What for?" asked Sonia amazed. Her recent meeting with his mother and sister had left a great impression which she could not analyze. She heard his news almost with horror.

"I have only you now," he added. "Let us go together . . . I've come to you, we are both accursed, let us go our way together!"

His eyes glittered "as though he were mad," Sonia thought, in her turn.

"Go where?" she asked in alarm, and she involuntarily stepped back.

"How do I know? I only know it's the same road, I know that and nothing more. It's the same goal!"

She looked at him and understood nothing. She knew only that he was terribly, infinitely unhappy.

"No one of them will understand, if you tell them, but I have understood. I need you, that is why I have come to you."

"I don't understand," whispered Sonia.

"You'll understand later. Haven't you done the same? You too have transgressed . . . have had the strength to transgress. You have laid hands on yourself, you have destroyed a life . . . *your own* (it's all the same!) You might have lived in spirit and understanding, but you'll end up going on the stage . . . But you won't be able to stand it, and if you remain alone you'll go out of your mind like me. You are like a mad creature already. So we must go together on the same road! Let us go!"

"What for? What's all this for?" said Sonia, strangely and violently agitated by his words.

"What for? Because you can't remain like this, that's why! You must look things straight in the face at last, and not weep like a child and cry that God won't allow it. What will happen if you should really be taken to the hospital tomorrow? She is mad and in consumption, she'll soon die, but the children? Do you mean to tell me Polenka won't come to grief? Haven't you seen children here at the street corners sent out by their mothers to beg? I've found out where those mothers live and in what surroundings. Children can't remain children there! At seven the child is vicious and a thief. Yet children, you know, are the image of Christ: 'Theirs is the kingdom of Heaven.' He bade us honor and love them, they are the humanity of the future . . .''

"What's to be done, what's to be done?" repeated Sonia, weeping hysterically and wringing her hands.

"What's to be done? Break what must be broken, once for all, that's all, and take the suffering on oneself. What, you don't understand? You'll understand later . . . Freedom and power, and above all, power! Over all trembling creation and all the ant heap! . . . That's the goal, remember that! That's my farewell message. Perhaps it's the last time I shall speak to you. If I don't come tomorrow, you'll hear of it all, and then remember these words. And some day later on, in years to come, you'll understand perhaps what they meant. If I come tomorrow, I'll tell you who killed Lizaveta . . . Good-bye."

Sonia started with terror.

"Why, do you know who killed her?" she asked, chilled with horror, looking wildly at him.

"I know and will tell . . . you, only you. I have chosen you out. I'm not coming to you to ask forgiveness, but simply to tell you. I chose you out long ago to hear this, when your father talked of you, and when Lizaveta was alive I thought of it. Goodbye, don't shake hands. Tomorrow!"

He went out. Sonia gazed at him as at a madman. But she herself was like one insane and felt it. Her head was going round.

"Good heavens, how does he know who killed Lizaveta? What did those words mean? It's awful!" But at the same time *the idea* did not enter her head, not for a moment! "Oh, he must be terribly unhappy! . . . He has abandoned his mother and sister . . . What for? What has happened? And what had he in his mind? What did he say to her? He had kissed her feet and said . . . said (yes, he had said it clearly) that he could not live without her . . . Oh, merciful heavens!''

Sonia spent the whole night feverish and delirious. She jumped up from time to time, wept and wrung her hands, then sank again into feverish sleep and dreamt of Polenka, Katerina Ivanovna, and Lizaveta, of reading the gospel and of him . . . him with pale face, with burning eyes . . . kissing her feet, weeping.

Hymn of the Men Underground

These words are spoken by Dmitri (Mitya) Karamazov who was unjustly accused of murdering his father and sentenced to twenty years of forced labor in Siberia. (More fully explained in the introductory paragraphs on page 58.) Precisely through this terrible fate he found the way back to God. He had never actually denied God; his sinful passions had only kept him far from Him. This passionate outburst is poured out to Dmitri's half-brother Alyosha (Alexey) when Alyosha visits Dmitri once more in prison just before he is deported to Siberia. Rakitin, the seminary student mentioned here, plays only the role of adversary in the novel; that is, an unscrupulous, career- and material-minded person.

Dmitri went up to Alyosha excitedly and kissed him. His eyes glowed.

"Rakitin wouldn't understand it," he began in a sort of exaltation, "but you, you'll understand it all. That's why I was thirsting for you. You see, there's so much I've been wanting to tell you for ever so long here, within these peeling walls, but I haven't said a word about what matters most; the moment never seems to have come. Now I can wait no longer. I must pour out my heart to you. Brother, these last two months I've found in myself a new man. A new man has risen up in me. He was hidden in me, but he would never have come to the surface if it hadn't been for this blow from heaven. I am afraid! And what do I care if I spend twenty years in the mines, breaking out ore with a hammer? I am not a bit afraid

142

of that — it's something else I am afraid of now: that that new man may leave me. Even there in the mines, underground, I may find a human heart in another convict and murderer by my side, and I may make friends with him, for even there one may live and love and suffer. One may thaw and revive a frozen heart in that convict, one may wait upon him for years, and at last bring up from the dark depths a lofty soul, a feeling, suffering creature; one may bring forth an angel, create a hero! There are so many of them, hundreds of them, and we are all to blame for them.

Why was it I dreamed of that 'babe' at such a moment? Why is the babe so poor? That was a sign to me at that moment. It's for the babe I'm going. Because we are all responsible for all. For all the 'babes,' for there are big children as well as little children. All are 'babes.' I go for all, because someone must go for all. I didn't kill father, but I've got to go. I accept it. It's all come to me here, here, within these peeling walls. There are numbers of them there, hundreds of them underground, with hammers in their hands. Oh, yes, we shall be in chains and there will be no freedom, but then in our great sorrow, we shall rise again to joy, without which man cannot live nor God exist, for God gives joy: it's His privilege — a grand one. Ah, man should be dissolved in prayer! What should I be underground there without God? Rakitin's lying! If they drive God from the earth, we shall shelter Him underground. One cannot exist in prison without God; it's even more impossible in prison than out. And then we men underground will sing from the bowels of the earth a glorious hymn to God, with Whom is joy. Hail to God and His joy! I love Him!''

Mitya was almost gasping for breath as he uttered his wild speech. He turned pale, his lips quivered, and tears rolled down his cheeks.

''Yes, life is full, there is life even underground,'' he

began again. "You wouldn't believe, Alexey, how I want to live now, what a thirst for existence and consciousness has sprung up in me within these peeling walls. Rakitin doesn't understand that; all he cares about is building a house and letting flats. But I've been longing for you. And what is suffering? I am not afraid of it, even if it were beyond reckoning. I am not afraid of it now. I was afraid of it before. Do you know, perhaps I won't answer at the trial at all . . . And I seem to have such strength in me now that I think I could stand anything, any suffering, only to be able to say and to repeat to myself every moment, 'I exist.' In thousands of agonies — I exist. I'm tormented on the rack — but I exist! Though I sit alone in darkness — I exist! I see the sun, and if I don't see the sun, I know it's there. And there's a whole life in that, in knowing that the sun is there. Alyosha, my angel, all these philosophies are the death of me. Damn them! Brother Ivan . . ."

"What of brother Ivan?" interrupted Alyosha, but Mitya did not hear.

"You see, I never had any of these doubts before, but it was all hidden away in me. It was perhaps just because I did not understand these ideas surging up in me that I used to drink and fight and rage. It was to stifle them in myself, to still them, to smother them. There is an idea in Ivan; he is not Rakitin. But Ivan is a sphinx and is silent; he is always silent. It's God that's worrying me. That's the only thing that's worrying me. What if He doesn't exist? What if Rakitin's right — that it's an idea made up by men? Then, if He doesn't exist, man is the chief of the earth, of the universe. Magnificent! Only how is he going to be good without God? That's the question. I always come back to that. For whom is man going to love then? To whom will he be thankful? To whom will he sing the hymn? Rakitin laughs, Rakitin says that one can love humanity without God. Well, only a sniveling idiot can maintain that. I can't understand it. Life's easy for Rakitin — 'You'd better think about the extension of civic rights,' he says, 'or even of keeping down the price of meat. You will show your love for humanity more simply and directly by that than by philosophy.' I answered him, 'Well, but you without a God, are more likely to raise the price of meat if it suits you and make a ruble on every kopeck.' He lost his temper. But after all, what is goodness? Answer me that, Alexey. Goodness is one thing with me and another with a Chinaman, so it's a relative thing. Or isn't it? Is it not relative? A treacherous question! You won't laugh if I tell you it's kept me awake two nights. I only wonder now how people can live and think nothing about it. Vanity! Ivan has no God. He has an idea.''

Reprieve and Execution

These two extracts are also from The Idiot. *"Reprieve" is a description by Prince Myshkin of the near execution of a political prisoner. Such a last-minute reprieve began Dostoyevsky's own ten-year period of imprisonment and exile with the drastic effect on his life described in the Introduction, page 15. "Execution" follows with an utter realism stemming from the inner experience of his own reprieve.*

REPRIEVE

"There may be two opinions about life in prison," said Myshkin. "A man who spent twelve years in prison told me his story. He was one of the invalids in the care of my professor. He had fits; he was sometimes restless, wept, and even tried to kill himself. His life in prison had been a very sad one, I assure you, but not at all petty. Yet he had no friends but a spider and a tree that grew under his window . . . But I'd better tell you how I met another man last year. There was one very strange circumstance about it — strange because such things rarely happen. This man had once been led out with others to the scaffold, and a sentence of death was read over him. He was to be shot for a political offence. Twenty moments later a reprieve was read to them, and they were condemned to another punishment instead. Yet the interval between those two sentences, twenty minutes or at least a

146

quarter of an hour, he passed in the fullest conviction that he would die in a few minutes.

"I was always eager to listen when he recalled his sensations at that time, and I often questioned him about it. He remembered it all with extraordinary distinctness and used to say that he never would forget those minutes. Twenty paces from the scaffold, round which soldiers and other people were standing, there were three posts stuck in the ground, as there were several criminals. The first three were led up, bound to the posts, the death garment (a long white gown) was put on, and white caps were pulled over their eyes so that they would not see the guns; then a company of several soldiers was drawn up against each post.

"My friend was the eighth on the list, so he had to be one of the third set. The priest went to each in turn with a cross. He had only five minutes more to live. He told me that those five minutes seemed to him an infinite time, a vast wealth; he felt that he had so many lives left in those five minutes that there was no need yet to think of the last moment, so much so that he divided his time up. He set aside time to take leave of his comrades, two minutes for that; then he kept another two minutes to think for the last time; and then a minute to look about him for the last time. He remembered very well having divided his time like that. He was dying at twenty-seven, strong and healthy. As he took leave of his comrades, he remembered asking one of them a somewhat irrelevent question and being particularly interested in the answer. Then when he had said good-bye, the two minutes came that he had set apart for *thinking* to himself. He knew beforehand what he would think about. He wanted to realize as quickly and clearly as possible how it could be that now he existed and was living and in three minutes he would be *something* — someone or something. But what? Where? He meant to decide all that in those two minutes!

"Not far off there was a church, and the gilt roof was glittering in the bright sunshine. He remembered that he stared very persistently at that roof and the light flashing from it; he could not tear himself away from the light. It seemed to him that those rays were his new nature and that in three minutes he would somehow melt into them . . . The uncertainty and feeling of aversion for that new thing which would be and was just coming was awful. But he said that nothing was so dreadful at that time as the continual thought, 'What if I were not to die! What if I could go back to life — what eternity! And it would all be mine! I would turn every minute into an age; I would lose nothing, I would count every minute as it passed, I would not waste one!' He said that this idea turned to such a fury at last that he longed to be shot quickly."

EXECUTION

"One thought came into my mind just now," Myshkin said to her, growing rather more animated again (he seemed easily roused to confiding animation), "when you asked me for a subject for a picture, to suggest that you should paint the face of the condemned man the moment before the blade falls, when he is still standing on the scaffold before he lies down on the plank."

"The face? The face alone?" asked Adelaïda. "That would be a strange subject. And what sort of picture would it make?"

"I don't know. Why not?" Myshkin insisted warmly. "I saw a picture like that at Basel not long ago. I should like to tell you about it . . . I'll tell you about it some day . . . It struck me very much."

"You shall certainly tell us afterwards about the picture at Basel," said Adelaïda; "and now explain the picture of this execution. Can you tell me how you imagine it to yourself? How is one to draw the face? Is it to be only the face? What sort of a face is it?"

"It's practically the minute before death," Myshkin began with perfect readiness, carried away by his memories and to all appearance instantly forgetting everything else, "that moment when he has just mounted the ladder and has just stepped onto the scaffold. Then he glanced in my direction. I looked at his face and I understood it all . . . But how can one describe it? I wish, I do wish that you or someone would paint it. It would be best if it were you. I thought at the time that a picture of it would do good. You know one has to imagine everything that has been before — everything, everything. He has been in prison awaiting execution for a week at least; he has been reckoning on the usual formalities, on the sentence being forwarded somewhere for signature and not coming back again for a week. But now by some chance this business was curtailed. At five o'clock in the morning he was asleep. It was at the end of October; at five o'clock it was still cold and dark. The superintendent of the prison came in quietly with the guard and touched him carefully on the shoulder. He sat up, leaning on his elbow, saw the light, asked 'What's the matter?' 'The execution is at ten o'clock.' He was half awake and couldn't take it in, and began objecting that the sentence wouldn't be ready for a week. But when he was fully awake he left off protesting and was silent — so I was told. Then he said, 'But it's hard it should be so sudden . . .' And again he was silent and wouldn't say anything more. The next three of four hours are spent on the usual things: seeing the priest, breakfast at which he is given wine, coffee, and beef (isn't that a mockery? Only think how cruel it is! Yet on the other hand, would you believe it, these innocent people act in good faith and are convinced that it's humane); then the toilet (do you know what a criminal's toilet is?); and at last they take him through the town to the scaffold . . . I think that he too must have thought he had an endless time left to live, while he was being driven through the town. He must have thought on the way, 'There's a long time left, three streets more. I shall pass through this one, then through the next, then there's that one left where there's a baker's on the right . . . It'll be a long time before we get to the baker's!'

"There were crowds of people, there was noise and shouting; ten thousand faces, ten thousand eyes — all that he has had to bear, and worst of all, the thought, 'They are ten thousand, but not one of them is being executed, and I am to be executed.' Well, all that is preparatory. There is a ladder to the scaffold. Suddenly at the foot of the ladder he began to cry, and he was a strong, manly fellow; he had been a great criminal, I was told. The priest never left him for a moment; he drove with him in the cart and talked with him all the while. I doubt whether he heard; he might have begun listening but not have understood more than two words. So it must have been. At last he began going up the ladder; his legs were fettered so that he could move with only short steps. The priest, who must have been an intelligent man, left off speaking and only gave him the cross to kiss. At the foot of the ladder he was very pale, and when he was at the top and standing on the scaffold, he became as white as paper, as white as writing paper. His legs must have grown weak and wooden, and I expect he felt sick — as though something were choking him and that made a sort of tickling in his throat. Have you ever felt that when you were frightened, or in awful moments when all your reason is left, but it has no power? I think that if one is faced by inevitable destruction — if a house is falling upon you, for instance — one must feel a great longing to sit down, close one's eyes and wait, come what may

. . . When that weakness was beginning, the priest with a rapid movement hastily put the cross to his lips — a little plain silver cross — he kept putting it to his lips every minute. And every time the cross touched his lips, he opened his eyes and seemed for a few seconds to come to life again, and his legs moved. He kissed the cross greedily; he made haste to kiss, as though in haste not to forget to provide himself with something in case of need; but I doubt whether he had any religious feeling at the time. And so it was till he was laid on the plank . . . It's strange that people rarely faint at these last moments. On the contrary, the brain is extraordinarily lively and must be working at a tremendous rate — at a tremendous rate, like a machine at full speed. I fancy that there is a continual throbbing of ideas of all sorts, always unfinished and perhaps absurd too, quite irrelevant ideas — 'That man is looking at me. He has a wart on his forehead. One of the executioner's buttons is rusty.' — and yet all the while one knows and remembers everything. There is one point which can never be forgotten, and one can't faint, and everything moves and turns about it, about that point. And only think that it must be like that up to the last quarter of a second, when his head lies on the block and he waits and . . . *knows*, and suddenly hears above him the clang of the iron! He must hear that! If I were lying there, I should listen on purpose and hear. It may last only the tenth part of a second, but one would be sure to hear it. And only fancy, it's still disputed whether, when the head is cut off, it knows for a second after that it has been cut off! What a thought! And what if it knows it for five seconds!

"Paint the scaffold so that only the last step can be distinctly seen in the foreground and the criminal having just stepped on it; his head, his face as white as paper; the priest holding up the cross, the man greedily putting forward his blue lips and looking — and aware of everything. The cross and the head — that's the picture. The priest's face and the executioner's, his two attendants and a few heads and eyes below might be painted in the background, in half light, as the setting . . . That's the picture!''

The Onion

In The Brothers Karamazov *this little story is told by Grushenka to Alyosha, whom she had tried to seduce but who not only had resisted her but even respected her sincerely as his equal and thus brought about her conversion and spiritual self-examination. This is typical of how redemption comes about in Dostoyevsky.*

Grushenka had been seduced as a young girl, abandoned, and then driven out of her parents' home. She lived in this town with her expenses paid by a rich old merchant whose mistress she had been. She had matured to rare beauty and from then on, until this experience with Alyosha, had sought to avenge herself at random on the whole world of men. The older Karamazov pursues her and so does Dmitri, who then succeeds just before his arrest in winning her sincere liking.

"Once upon a time there was a peasant woman, and a very wicked woman she was. And she died and did not leave a single good deed behind. The devils caught her and plunged her into the lake of fire. So her guardian angel stood and wondered what good deed of hers he could remember to tell to God. 'She once pulled up an onion in her garden,' said he, 'and gave it to a beggar woman.' And God answered: 'You take that onion then, hold it out to her in the lake, and let her take hold and be pulled out. And if you can pull her out of the lake, let her come to Paradise, but if the onion breaks, then the woman must stay where she is.' The angel ran to the woman and held out the onion to her: 'Come,' said he, 'catch

155

hold and I'll pull you out,' And he began cautiously pulling her out. He had almost pulled her right out, when the other sinners in the lake, seeing how she was being drawn out, began catching hold of her so as to be pulled out with her. But she was a very wicked woman and she began kicking them. 'I'm to be pulled out, not you. It's my onion, not yours,' As soon as she said that, the onion broke. And the women fell into the lake, and she is burning there to this day. So the angel wept and went away. So that's the story, Alyosha; I know it by heart, for I am that wicked woman myself."

The Last Judgment

This is a section of the description from Crime and Punishment *of Raskolnikov's meeting with Semyon Zaharovitch Marmeladov, father of the prostitute Sonia. The place of these main characters in the story is given in the introductory paragraphs on page 119.*

Marmeladov stopped again in violent excitement. At that moment a whole party of revelers already drunk came in from the street, and the sounds of a hired concertina and the cracked piping voice of a child of seven singing "The Homestead" were heard in the entry. The room was filled with noise. The tavern-keeper and the boys were busy with the newcomers. Marmeladov, paying no attention to the new arrivals, continued his story. He appeared by now to be extremely tipsy, but as he became more and more drunk, he became more and more talkative. The recollection of his recent success in getting his position back seemed to revive him and was reflected in a radiance on his face. Raskolnikov listened attentively.

"That was five weeks ago, sir. Yes . . . As soon as Katerina Ivanovna and Sonia heard of it, mercy on us, it was as though I stepped into the kingdom of Heaven. It used to be: "You can lie there like a beast" — nothing but abuse. Now they were walking on tiptoe, hushing the children. 'Semyon Zaharovitch is tired with his work at the office, he is resting, shh!' They made me coffee before I went to work and boiled cream for me! They began to get real cream for me, do you hear that? And how they managed to get together the money for a decent outfit — eleven rubles, fifty kopecks — I can't guess. Boots, cotton shirtfronts — most magnificent, a uniform, all got up in splendid style, for eleven rubles and a half. The first morning I came back from the office I found Katerina Ivanovna had cooked two courses for dinner — soup and salted meat with horseradish — which we had never dreamed of until then. She had no dresses, none at all, but she got herself up as if she were going on a visit — not that she'd anything to do it with. She smartened herself up with nothing at all: she'd done her hair nicely, put on a clean collar of some sort, cuffs, and there she was, quite a different person, younger and better looking. Sonia, my little darling, had only helped with money. 'For the time,' she said, 'it won't do for me to come and see you too often. After dark maybe when no one can see.' Do you hear, do you hear? I lay down for a nap after dinner and what do you think: though Katerina Ivanovna had absolutely broken off with our landlady Amalia Fyodorovna only a week before, she could not resist asking her in to coffee. For two hours they were sitting, whispering together: 'Semyon Zaharovitch is in the service again now and receiving a salary,' says she, 'and he went to his excellency, and his excellency himself came out to him, made all the others wait, and led Semyon Zaharovitch by the hand before everybody into his study.' — Do you hear, do you hear? — 'To be sure,' says he, 'Semyon Zaharovitch, remembering your past services,' says he, 'and in spite of your propensity to that foolish weakness, since you now give me your promise and, moreover, since we've got on badly without you,' — Do you hear, do you hear? — 'and so,' says he, 'I rely on your word as a gentleman.' And let me tell you, she has simply made up all that herself, and not simply out of silliness for the sake of bragging; no, she believes it all herself, she amuses herself with her own fancies; upon my word, she does!

And I don't blame her for it, no, I don't blame her! . . . Six days ago when I brought her my first earnings in full — twenty-three rubles forty kopecks altogether — she called me her poppet: 'Poppet,' said she, 'my little poppet.' And when we were by ourselves, you understand? You would not think me a beauty, you would not think much of me as a husband, would you? . . . Well, she pinched my cheek. 'My little poppet,' said she."

Marmeladov broke off, tried to smile, but suddenly his chin began to twitch. He controlled himself however. The tavern, the degraded appearance of the man, the five nights in the hay barge, and the jug of spirits, and yet this poignant love for his wife and children bewildered his listener. Raskolnikov listened intently but with a sick sensation. He felt vexed that he had come here.

"Honored sir, honored sir," cried Marmeladov recovering himself — "Oh, sir, perhaps all this seems a laughing matter to you, as it does to others, and perhaps I am only worrying you with the stupidity of all the trivial details of my home life, but it is not a laughing matter to me. For I can feel it all . . . And the whole of that heavenly day of my life and the whole of that evening I passed in fleeting dreams of how I would arrange it all, how I would dress all the children, how I would give her rest, and how I would rescue my own daughter from dishonor and restore her to the bosom of her family . . . And a great deal more . . . Quite excusable, sir. Well then, sir (Marmeladov suddenly gave a sort of start, raised his head, and gazed intently at his listener), well, on the very next day after all those dreams (that is to say, exactly five days ago in the evening) by a cunning trick, like a thief in the night, I stole from Katerina Ivanovna the key of her box, took out what was left of my earnings — how much it was I have forgotten — and now look at me, all of you! It's the fifth day since I left home, and they are looking for me there, and it's the end of my employment, and my uniform is lying in a tavern on the Egyptian bridge. I exchanged it for the garments I have on . . . and it's the end of everything!"

Marmeladov struck his forehead with his fist, clenched his teeth, closed his eyes, and leaned heavily with his elbow on the table. But a minute later his face suddenly changed and with a certain assumed slyness and affectation of bravado, he glanced at Raskolnikov, laughed and said:

"This morning I went to see Sonia and to ask her for a pick-me-up! He-he-he!"

"You don't say she gave it to you? cried one of the newcomers; he shouted the words and went off into a guffaw.

"This very quart was bought with her money," Marmeladov declared, addressing himself exclusively to Raskolnikov. "Thirty kopecks she gave me with her own hands, her last, all she had, as I saw . . . She said nothing, she only looked at me without a word . . . Not on earth, but up yonder . . . they grieve over men, they weep, but they don't blame them, they don't blame them! But it hurts more, it hurts more when they don't blame! Thirty kopecks yes! And maybe she needs them now, eh? What do you think, my dear sir? For now she's got to keep up her appearance. It costs money, that smartness, that special smartness, you know? Do you understand? And there's haircream too, you see, she must have things; petticoats, starched ones, shoes too, really trim ones to show off her foot when she has to step over a puddle. Do you understand, sir, do you understand what all that smartness means? And here I, her own father, here I took thirty kopecks of that money for a drink! And I am drinking it! And I have already drunk it! Come, who will have pity on a man like me, eh? Are you sorry for me, sir, or not? Tell me sir, are you sorry or not? He-he-he!"

He would have filled his glass, but there was no drink left. The jug was empty.

"What are you to be pitied for?" shouted the tavern-keeper, who was again near them.

Shouts of laughter and even oaths followed. The laughter and the oaths came from those who were listening and also from those who had heard nothing but were simply looking at the figure of the discharged government clerk.

"To be pitied! Why am I to be pitied?" Marmeladov suddenly declaimed standing up with his arm outstretched, as though he had been only waiting for that question.

"Why am I to be pitied, you say? Yes! There's nothing to pity me for! I ought to be crucified, crucified, not pitied! Crucify me, O judge, crucify me, but pity me! And then I will go of myself to be crucified, for it's not merry-making I seek, but tears and tribulation! . . . Do you suppose, you that sell, that this pint of yours has been sweet to me? It was tribulation I sought at the bottom of it, tears and tribulation, and have found it, and I have tasted it; but He will pity us Who has had pity on all men, Who has understood all men and all things, He is the One, He too is the judge. He will come in that day and He will ask: 'Where is the daughter who gave herself for her angry, consumptive stepmother and for the little children of another? Where is the daughter who had pity upon the filthy drunkard, her earthly father, undismayed by his beastliness?' And He will say, 'Come to me! I have already forgiven thee once . . . Thy sins which are many are forgiven thee, for thou hast loved much . . .' And He will forgive my Sonia, He will forgive, I know it . . . I felt it in my heart when I was with her just now! And He will judge and will forgive all, the good and the evil, the wise and the meek . . . And when He has done with all of them, then He will summon us. 'You too come forth,' He will say, 'Come forth, ye drunkards, come forth, ye weak ones, come forth, ye children of shame!' And we shall all come forth without shame and shall stand before Him. And He will say unto us, 'Ye are swine, made in the image of the Beast and with his mark; but come ye also!' And the wise ones and those of understanding will say, 'O Lord, why dost Thou receive these men?' And He will say, 'This is why I receive them, O ye wise, this is why I receive them, O ye of understanding, that not one of them believed himself to be worthy of this.' And He will hold out His hands to us and we shall fall down before Him . . . and we shall weep . . . and we shall understand all things! Then we shall understand all! . . . and all will understand, Katerina Ivanovna even . . . she will understand . . . Lord, Thy kingdom come!''' And he sank down on the bench exhausted and helpless, looking at no one, apparently oblivious of his surroundings and plunged in deep thought. His words had created a certain impression; there was a moment of silence; but soon laughter and oaths were heard again.

The Crucifixion

Holbein's painting, "Christ Taken Down From the Cross," inspired this description taken from The Idiot. *A copy of the painting hanging in Rogozhin's house is first mentioned in an exchange between him and Prince Myshkin over its effect on their faith. The impression the original made on Dostoyevsky is more fully told in the Foreword.*

The question of faith also ends this extract about the painting, a description taken out of a long statement written by Ippolit (the young consumptive protégé of Myshkin). He entitled his statement "A Necessary Explanation" and read it aloud to a gathering in Lebedyev's house just before making an unsuccessful attempt to shoot himself.

"The picture depicted Christ who has only just been taken down from the cross. I believe artists usually paint Christ, both on the cross and after He has been taken from the cross, still with extraordinary beauty of face. They strive to preserve that beauty even in His most terrible agonies. In Rogozhin's picture there's no trace of beauty. It is in every detail the corpse of a man who has endured infinite agony before the crucifixion; who has been wounded, tortured, beaten by the guards and the people when He carried the cross on His back and fell beneath its weight, and after that has undergone the agony of crucifixion, lasting for six hours at least (according to my reckoning). It's true it's the face of a man *only just* taken from the cross — that is to say, still bearing traces of warmth and life. Nothing is rigid in it yet, so that there's still a look of suffering in the face of the dead man, as though he were still feeling it (that has been very well caught by the artist). Yet the face has not been spared in the least. It is simply nature, and the corpse of a man, whoever he might be, must really look like that after such suffering. I know that the Christian Church laid it down, even in the early ages, that Christ's suffering was not symbolical but actual, and that His body was therefore fully and completely subject to the laws of nature on the cross. In the picture the face is fearfully crushed by blows, swollen, covered with fearful, swollen, and blood-stained bruises, the eyes are open and squinting: the great wide-open whites of the eyes glitter with a sort of deathly, glassy light. But, strange to say, as one looks at this corpse of a tortured man, a peculiar and curious question arises; if just such a corpse (and it must have been just like that) was seen by all His disciples, by those who were to become His chief apostles, by the women that followed Him and stood by the cross, by all who believed in Him and worshiped Him, how could they believe that that martyr would rise again? The question, instinctively arises: if death is so awful and the laws of nature so mighty, how can they be overcome? How can they be overcome when even He did not conquer them, He who vanquished nature in His lifetime, who exclaimed, 'Maiden, arise!' and the maiden arose — 'Lazarus, come forth!' and the dead man came forth? Looking at such a picture, one conceives of nature in the shape of an immense, merciless, dumb beast, or more correctly, much more correctly, speaking, though it sounds strange, in the form of a huge machine of the most modern construction which, dull and insensible, has aimlessly clutched, crushed, and swallowed up a great priceless Being, a Being worth all nature and its laws, worth the whole earth, which was created perhaps solely for the sake of the advent of that Being. This picture expresses and unconsciously suggests to one the conception of such a dark, insolent, unreasoning, and eternal

Power to which everything is in subjection. The people sur-
rounding the dead man, not one of whom is shown in the
picture, must have experienced the most terrible anguish and
consternation on that evening, which had crushed all their
hopes and almost their convictions. They must have parted in
the most awful terror, though each one bore within him a
mighty thought which could never be wrested from him. And
if the Teacher could have seen Himself on the eve of the
crucifixion, would He have gone up to the cross and have died
as He did? That question too rises involuntarily, as one looks
at the picture.

From the Life of the Elder Zossima

These are episodes from The Brothers Karamazov, *entirely independent and complete in themselves. Zossima is a very strict and most highly esteemed monk, a recluse, of the kind called starets (elder), and at the same time the spiritual father and eternal example for Alyosha (Alexey) Fyodorovitch Karamazov. Just before Zossima dies, he tells his friends, the monks, how he found the way to God, and this is taken down by Alyosha.*

FATHER ZOSSIMA'S BROTHER

Beloved fathers and teachers, I was born in a distant province in the north, in the town of V. My father was a gentleman by birth but of no great consequence or position. He died when I was only two years old, and I don't remember him at all. He left my mother a small house built of wood, and some capital — not much but sufficient to keep her and her children in comfort. There were two of us, my elder brother Markel and I. He was eight years older than I was, of hasty, irritable temperament but kindhearted and never ironical. He was remarkably silent, especially at home with me, his mother, and the servants. He did well at school but did not get on with his schoolfellows, though he never quarrelled — at least so my mother has told me. Six months before his death, when he was seventeen, he made friends with a political exile who had been banished to our town from Moscow for free-thinking and led a solitary existence there. He was a good scholar who had gained distinction in philosophy in the university. Something made him take a fancy to Markel, and he would ask him to see him. The young man spent whole evenings with him during that winter, till the exile was summoned to Petersburg to take up his post again at his own request, as he had powerful friends.

It was the beginning of Lent, and Markel would not fast; he was rude and laughed at it. "That's all silly twaddle and there is no God," he said, horrifying my mother, the servants, and me too. For though I was only nine, I too was aghast at hearing such words. We had four servants, all serfs. I remember my mother selling one of the four, the cook Afymya, who was lame and elderly, for sixty paper rubles, and hiring a free servant to take her place.

In the sixth week in Lent my brother, who was never strong and had a tendency to consumption, was taken ill. He was tall but thin and delicate-looking and of very pleasing countenance. I suppose he caught cold; anyway the doctor who came soon whispered to my mother that it was galloping consumption, that he would not live through the spring. My mother began weeping, and careful not to alarm my brother, she entreated him to go to church, to confess, and take the sacrament, for he was still able to move about. This made him angry, and he said something profane about the church. He grew thoughtful, however; he guessed at once that he was seriously ill, and that that was why his mother was begging him to confess and take the sacrament. He had been aware, indeed for a long time past, that he was far from well and had just a year before coolly observed at dinner to our mother and me, "My life won't be long among you; I may not live another year," which seemed now like a prophecy.

Three days passed and Holy Week had come. And on Tuesday morning my brother began going to church. "I am doing this simply for your sake, mother, to please and comfort you," he said. My mother wept with joy and grief. "His end must be near," she thought, "if there's such a change in him." But he was not able to go to church long, he took to his bed, so he had to confess and take the sacrament at home.

It was a late Easter, and the days were bright, fine, and full of fragrance. I remember he used to cough all night and sleep badly, but in the morning he dressed and tried to sit up in an armchair. That's how I remember him sitting — sweet and gentle, smiling, his face bright and joyous in spite of his illness. A marvelous change passed over him, his spirit seemed transformed. The old nurse would come in and say, "Let me light the lamp before the holy image, my dear." Earlier he would not have allowed it and would have blown it out.

"Light it, light it, dear, I was a wretch to have prevented you doing it. You are praying when you light the lamp, and I am praying when I rejoice seeing you. So we are praying to the same God."

Those words seemed strange to us, and mother would go to her room and weep, but when she went in to him she wiped her eyes and looked cheerful. "Mother, don't weep, darling," he would say, "I've long to live yet, long to rejoice with you, and life is glad and joyful."

"Ah, dear boy, how can you talk of joy when you lie feverish at night, coughing as though you would tear yourself to pieces."

"Don't cry, mother," he would answer, "life is paradise, and we are all in paradise, but we will not see it; if we would, we should have heaven on earth the same day."

Every one wondered at his words, he spoke so strangely and positively; we were all touched and wept. Friends came to see us. "Dear ones," he would say to them, "what have I done that you should love me so, how can you love anyone like me, and how was it I did not know, I did not appreciate it before?"

When the servants came in to him, he would say continually, "Dear, kind people, why are you doing so much for me, do I deserve to be waited on? If it were God's will for me to live, I would wait on you, for all men should wait on one another."

Mother shook her head as she listened. "My darling, it's your illness makes you talk like that."

"Mother, darling," he would say, "there must be servants and masters, but if so, I will be the servant of my servants, the same as they are to me. And another thing, mother, everyone of us has sinned against all men and I more than any."

Mother positively smiled at that, smiled through her tears. "Why, how could you have sinned against all men, more than all? Robbers and murderers have done that, but what sin have you committed yet that you hold yourself more guilty than all?"

"Mother, little heart of mine," he said (he had begun using such strange caressing words at that time), "little heart of mine, my joy, believe me, every one is really responsible to all men for all men and for everything. I don't know how to explain it to you, but I feel it is so, painfully so. And how is it we then went on living, getting angry and not knowing?"

So he would get up every day, more and more sweet and joyous and full of love. When the doctor, an old German called Eisenschmidt, came he would ask jokingly: "Well, doctor, have I another day in this world?"

"You'll live many days yet," the doctor would answer, "and months and years too."

"Months and years!" he would exclaim. "Why reckon the days? One day is enough for a man to know all happiness. My dear ones, why do we quarrel, try to outshine each other, and keep grudges against each other? Let's go straight into the garden, walk and play there, love, appreciate, and kiss each other, and glorify life."

"Your son cannot last long," the doctor told my mother, as she accompanied him to the door. "The disease is affecting his brain."

The windows of his room looked out into the garden, and our garden was a shady one, with old trees in it which were coming into bud. The first birds of spring were flitting in the branches, chirruping and singing at the windows. And looking at them and admiring them, he began suddenly begging their forgiveness too, "Birds of heaven, happy birds, forgive me: for I have sinned against you too." None of us could understand that at the time, but he shed tears of joy. "Yes," he said, "there was always such a glory of God all about me, birds, trees, meadows, sky, only I lived in shame and dishonored it all and did not notice the beauty and glory."

"You take too many sins on yourself," mother used to say, weeping.

"Mother, darling, it's for joy, not for grief I am crying. Though I can't explain it to you, I like to humble myself before them, for I don't know how to love them enough. If I have sinned against every one, yet all forgive me too, and that's heaven. Am I not in heaven now?"

And there was a great deal more I don't remember. I remember I once went into his room when there was no one else there. It was a bright evening, the sun was setting, and the whole room was lighted up. He beckoned me, and I went up to him. He put his hands on my shoulders and looked into my face tenderly, lovingly; he said nothing for a minute, only looked at me like that.

"Well," he said, "run and play now, enjoy life for me too." I went out then and ran to play. And many times in my life afterwards I remembered even with tears how he told me to enjoy life for him too. There were many other marvelous and beautiful sayings of his, though we did not understand them at the time. He died the third week after Easter. He was fully conscious though he could not talk; up to his last hour he did not change. He looked happy, his eyes beamed and sought us, he smiled at us, beckoned us. There was a great deal of talk even in the town about his death. I was impressed by all this at the time, but not too much so, though I cried a great deal at his funeral. I was young then, a child; but a lasting impression remained in my heart, a hidden feeling of it, all ready to rise up and respond when the time came. And indeed it happened.

THE HOLY SCRIPTURES IN THE LIFE OF FATHER ZOSSIMA

I was left alone with my mother. Her friends began advising her to send me to Petersburg as other parents did. "You have only one son now," they said, "and have a fair income, and you will perhaps be depriving him of a brilliant career if you keep him here." They suggested I should be sent to Petersburg to the Cadet Corps so that I might afterward enter the Imperial Guard. My mother hesitated for a long time; it was awful to part with her only child, but she made up her mind to it at last, though not without many tears, believing she was acting for my happiness. She brought me to Petersburg and put me into the Cadet Corps, and I never saw her again, for she died three years afterward. She spent those three years mourning and grieving for both of us.

From the house of my childhood I have brought nothing but precious memories, for there are no memories more precious than those of early childhood in one's first home. And that is almost always so if there is any love and harmony in the family at all. Indeed, precious memories may remain even of a bad home, if only the heart knows how to find what is precious. With my memories of home I include my memories of the Bible, which child as I was I was very eager to read at home. I had then a book of Bible stories with excellent pictures called "A Hundred and Four Stories from the Old and New Testament," and I learned to read from it. I have it lying on my shelf now; I keep it as a precious relic of the past. But even before I learned to read, I remember first being moved to a feeling of devotion at eight years of age. My mother took me alone to mass — I don't remember where my brother was at the time — on the Monday before Easter. It was a fine day, and I remember it as though I saw it now, how the incense rose from the censer and softly floated upwards and, overhead in the cupola, mingled in rising waves with the sunlight that streamed in at the little window. I was stirred by the sight, and for the first time in my life I consciously received the seed of God's word in my heart. A youth came out into the middle of the church carrying a big book, so large that at the time I fancied he could scarcely carry it. He laid it on the reading desk, opened it, and began reading, and suddenly for the first time I understood something read in the church of God.

In the land of Uz, there lived a man, righteous and God-fearing, and he had great wealth — so many camels, so many sheep and asses — and his children feasted, and he loved them very much and prayed for them: "It may be that my sons have sinned in their feasting." Now the devil came before the Lord together with the sons of God and said to the Lord that he had gone up and down the earth and under the earth. "And hast thou considered my servant Job?" God asked of him. And God boasted to the devil, pointing to His great and holy servant. And the devil laughed at God's words. "Give him over to me and Thou wilt see that Thy servant will murmur against Thee and curse Thy name." And God gave up the just man He loved so well to the devil. And the devil smote his children and his cattle and scattered his wealth, all of a sudden like a thunderbolt from heaven. And Job rent his mantle and fell down upon the ground and cried aloud, "Naked came I out of my mother's womb, and naked shall I return into the earth; the Lord gave and the Lord has taken away. Blessed be the name of the Lord for ever and ever."

Fathers and teachers, forgive my tears now, for all my childhood rises up again before me, and I breathe now as I breathed then, with the breast of a little child of eight, and I feel as I did then, awe and wonder and gladness. The camels at that time caught my imagination, and Satan who talked like that with God, and God who gave His servant up to destruction, and His servant who cried out: "Blessed be Thy name although Thou dost punish me," and then the soft and sweet singing in the church: "Let my prayer rise up before Thee," and again incense from the priest's censer and the kneeling and the prayer. Ever since then — only yesterday I took it up — I've never been able to read that sacred tale without tears. And how much that is great, mysterious, and unfathomable there is in it! Afterward I heard the words of mockery and blame, proud words. "How could God give up the most loved of His saints for the diversion of the devil, take from him his children, smite him with sore boils so that he cleansed the corruption from his sores with a potsherd — and for no object except to boast to the devil? 'See what My saint can suffer for My sake.'"

But the greatness of it lies just in the fact that it is a mystery — that the passing earthly show and the eternal verity are brought together in it. In the face of earthly truth, the eternal truth is accomplished. Just as on the first days of creation the Creator ended each day with praise, saying "What I have created is good," so now He looks upon Job and again praises His creation. And Job praising the Lord, serves not only Him but all His creation for generations and generations and for ever and ever, since for that he was ordained.

Good heavens, what a book it is, and what lessons there are in it! What a book the Bible is, what a miracle, what strength is given with it to man. It is like a mold cast of the world and man and human nature, everything is there, and a law for everything for all the ages. And what mysteries are solved and revealed; God raises Job again, gives him wealth again. Many years pass by, and he has other children and loves them. But how could he love those new ones when those first children are no more, when he has lost them? Remembering them, how could he be fully happy with those new ones, however dear the new ones might be? But he could, he could. It's the great mystery of human life that old grief passes gradually into quiet, tender joy. The mild serenity of age takes the place of the riotous blood of youth. I bless the rising sun each day, and as before, my heart sings to meet it, but now I love even more its setting, its long slanting rays and the soft, tender, gentle memories that come with them, the dear images from the whole of my long happy life — and over all the Divine Truth, softening, reconciling, forgiving! My life is ending, I know that well, but every day that is left me I feel how my earthly life is in touch with a new, infinite, unknown, but approaching life, the nearness of which sets my soul quivering with rapture, my mind glowing and my heart weeping with joy.

Friends and teachers, I have heard more than once, and of late one may hear it more often, that the priests, and above all the village priests, are complaining on all sides of their miserable income and their humiliating lot. They plainly state, even in print — I've read it myself — that they are unable to teach the Scriptures to the people because of the smallness of their means, and if Lutherans and heretics come and lead the flock astray, they let them lead them astray because they have so little to live upon. May the Lord increase the sustenance that is so precious to them, for their complaint is also just. But of a truth I say, if anyone is to blame in the matter, half the fault is ours. For he may be short of time, he may say truly that he is overwhelmed all the while with work and services, but still it's not all the time, even he has an hour a week to remember God. And he does not work the whole year round. If at first he gathers only the children — once a week, some hour in the evening — the fathers will hear of it and they too will begin to come. There's no need to build halls for this, let him take them into his own cottage. They won't spoil his cottage; they would only be there one hour. Let him open that book and begin reading it without grand words or superciliousness, without condescension to them but gently and kindly, being glad that he is reading to them and that they are listening with attention, loving the words himself, only stopping from time to time to explain words that are not understood by the peasants. Don't be anxious, they will understand everything; the orthodox heart will understand all! Let him read them about Abraham and Sarah, about Isaac and Rebecca, of how Jacob went to Laban and wrestled with the Lord in his dream and said, ''This place is holy'' — and he will impress the devout mind of the peasant. Let him read, especially to the children, how the brothers sold Joseph — the tender boy, the dreamer and prophet — into bondage and told their father that a wild beast had devoured him and showed him his blood-stained clothes.

Let him read them how the brothers afterward journeyed into Egypt for wheat and how Joseph, already a great ruler, unrecognized by them, tormented them, accused them, kept his brother Benjamin, and all through love: ''I love you, and loving you I torment you.'' For he remembered all his life how they had sold him to the merchants in the burning desert by the well and how, wringing his hands, he had wept and besought his brothers not to sell him as a slave in a strange land. And how, seeing them again after many years, he loved them beyond measure, but he harassed and tormented them in love. He left them at last not able to bear the suffering of his heart, flung himself on his bed and wept. Then, wiping his tears away he went out to them joyful and told them: "Brothers, I am your brother Joseph!" Let him read them further how happy old Jacob was on learning that his darling boy was still alive and how he went to Egypt, leaving his own country, and died in a foreign land, bequeathing his great prophecy that had lain mysteriously hidden in his meek and timid heart all his life: that from his offspring, from Judah, will come the great hope of the world, the Messiah and Savior.

Fathers and teachers, forgive me and don't be angry that like a little child I've been babbling of what you know from long ago and can teach me a hundred times more skillfully. I only speak from rapture, and forgive my tears, for I love the Bible. Let him too weep, the priest of God, and be sure that the hearts of his listeners will throb in response. Only a little tiny seed is needed — drop it into the heart of the peasant and it won't die, it will live in his soul all his life, it will be hidden in the midst of his darkness and sin, like a bright spot, like a great reminder. And there's no need of much teaching or explanation; he will understand it all simply. Do you suppose that the peasants don't understand? Try reading them the touching story of the fair Esther and the haughty Vashti; or the miraculous story of Jonah in the whale. Don't forget either the parables of Our Lord; choose especially from the Gospel of St. Luke — that is what I did — and then from the Acts of the Apostles the conversion of St. Paul — that you mustn't leave out on any account — and from the Lives of the Saints — for instance the life of Alexey, the man of God — and, greatest of all, the happy martyr and the bearer of God, Mary of Egypt — and you will penetrate their hearts with these simple tales. Give one hour a week to it in spite of your poverty, only one little hour. And you will see for yourself that our people are gracious and grateful and will repay you a hundredfold. Mindful of the kindness of their priest and the moving words they have heard from him, they will of their own accord help him in his fields and in his house and will treat him with more respect than before — so that it will even increase his worldly well-being too. The thing is so simple that sometimes one is even afraid to put it into words for fear of being laughed at, and yet how true it is! One who does not believe in God will not believe in God's people. He who believes in God's people will see His Holiness too, even though he had not believed in it till then. Only the people and their future spiritual power will convert our atheists, who have torn themselves away from their native soil.

And what is the use of Christ's words unless we set an example? The people are lost without the word of God, for their soul is athirst for the Word and for all that is good.

In my youth long ago, nearly forty years ago, I traveled all over Russia with Father Anfim, collecting funds for our monastery, and we stayed one night on the bank of a great navigable river with some fishermen. A good-looking peasant lad, about eighteen, joined us; he had to hurry back next morning to pull a merchant's barge along the bank. I noticed him looking straight before him with clear and tender eyes. It was a bright, warm, still July night, a cool mist rose from the broad river, we could hear the splash of a fish, the birds were still, all was hushed and beautiful, everything praying to God. Only we two were not sleeping, the lad and I, and we talked of the beauty of this world of God's and of the great mystery of it. Every blade of grass, every insect, ant, and golden bee, all so marvelously know their path; though they have not intelligence, they bear witness to the mystery of God and continually accomplish it themselves. I saw the dear lad's heart was moved. He told me that he loved the forest and the forest birds. He was a bird catcher, knew the note of each of them, could call each bird. "I know nothing better than to be in the forest," said he, "though all things are good."

"Truly," I answered him, "all things are good and fair, because all is truth. Look," said I, "at the horse, that great beast that is so near to man; or the lowly, pensive ox, which feeds him and works for him; look at their faces, what meekness, what devotion to man, who often beats them mercilessly. What gentleness, what confidence and what beauty! It's touching to know that there's no sin in them; for all, all except man, are sinless, and Christ has been with them before us."

"Why," asked the boy, "is Christ with them too?"

"It cannot but be so," said I, "since the Word is for all. All creation and all creatures, every leaf is striving toward the Word, singing glory to God, weeping to Christ, unconsciously accomplishing this by the mystery of their sinless life. Yonder," said I, "in the forest wanders the dreadful bear, fierce and menacing, and yet innocent in it." And I told him how once a bear came to a great saint who had taken refuge in a tiny cell in the wood. And the great saint pitied him, went up to him without fear, and gave him a piece of bread. "Go along," said he, "Christ be with you," and the savage beast walked away meekly and obediently, doing no harm. And the lad was delighted that the bear had walked away without hurting the saint and that Christ was with him too. "Ah," said he, "how good that is, how good and beautiful is all God's work!" He sat musing softly and sweetly. I saw he understood. And he slept beside me a light and sinless sleep. May God bless youth! And I prayed for him as I went to sleep. Lord, send peace and light to Thy people!

RECOLLECTIONS OF FATHER ZOSSIMA'S YOUTH
BEFORE HE BECAME A MONK. THE DUEL

I spent a long time, almost eight years, in the Cadet Corps at Petersburg, and in the novelty of my surroundings there, many of my childish impressions grew dimmer, though I forgot nothing. I picked up so many new habits and opinions that I was transformed into a cruel, absurd, almost savage creature. A surface polish of courtesy and society manners I did acquire together with the French language.

But we all, myself included, looked upon the soldiers in our service as cattle. I was perhaps worse than the rest in that respect, for I was so much more impressionable than my companions. By the time we left the school as officers, we were ready to lay down our lives for the honor of the regiment, but no one of us had any knowledge of the real meaning of honor, and if anyone had known it, he would have been the first to ridicule it. Drunkenness, debauchery, and devilry were what we almost prided ourselves on. I don't say that we were bad by nature — all these young men were good fellows — but they behaved badly, and I worst of all. What made it worse for me was that I had come into my own money, and so I flung myself into a life of pleasure and plunged headlong into all the recklessness of youth.

I was fond of reading, yet strange to say, the Bible was the one book I never opened at that time, though I always carried it about with me and was never separated from it; in very truth I was keeping that book "for the day and the hour, for the month and the year" though I knew it not.

After four years of this life, I chanced to be in the town of K. where our regiment was stationed at the time. We found the people of the town hospitable, rich, and fond of entertainments. I met with a cordial reception everywhere, as I was of a lively temperament and was known to be well-off, which always goes a long way in the world. And then a circumstance happened that was the beginning of everything.

I formed an attachment to a beautiful and intelligent young girl of noble and lofty character, the daughter of people much respected. They were well-to-do people of influence and position. They always gave me a cordial and friendly reception. I fancied that the young lady looked on me with favor, and my heart was aflame at such an idea. Later on I saw and fully realized that I perhaps was not so passionately in love with her at all but only recognized the elevation of her mind and character, which I could not indeed have helped doing. I was prevented, however, from making her an offer at the time by my selfishness; I was loath to part with the allurements of my free and licentious bachelor life in the heyday of my youth and with my pockets full of money. I did drop some hint as to my feelings, however, though I put off taking any decisive step for a time. Then, all of a sudden, we were ordered off for two months to another district.

On my return two months later, I found the young lady already married to a rich neighboring landowner, a very amiable man, still young though older than I was, connected with the best Petersburg society, which I was not, and of excellent education, which I also was not. I was so shaken by this unexpected turn of events that I completely lost my head. The worst of it all was that, as I learned then, the young landowner had been betrothed to her a long while, and in fact I had met him many times in her house, but blinded by my conceit I had noticed nothing. And this particularly mortified me; almost everybody had known all about it, while I knew nothing. I was filled with sudden irrepressible fury. With flushed face I began recalling how often I had been on the point of declaring my love to her, and as she had not attempted to stop me or warn me, she must, I concluded, have been laughing at me all the time. Later on, of course, I reflected and remembered that she had been very far from laughing at me; on the contrary, she used to turn off any lovemaking on my part with a jest and begin talking of other subjects; but at that moment I was incapable of reflecting and was all eagerness for revenge. I am surprised to remember that my wrath and revengeful feelings were extremely repugnant to my own nature; for being of an easy temper, I found it difficult to be angry with anyone for long, and so I had to work myself up artificially and become at last revolting and absurd.

I waited for an opportunity and succeeded in insulting my "rival" in the presence of a large company. I insulted him on a perfectly extraneous pretext, jeering at his opinion upon an important public event — it was in the year 1826 — and my jeer was, so people said, clever and effective. Then I forced him to ask for an explanation and behaved so rudely that he accepted my challenge in spite of the vast inequality between us — I was younger, a person of no consequence, and of inferior rank. I learned afterward for a fact that it was from a jealous feeling on his side also that my challenge was accepted; he had been rather jealous of me on his wife's account before their marriage; he fancied now that if he submitted to be insulted by me and refused to accept any challenge, and if she heard of it, she might begin to despise him and waver in her love for him. I soon found a second in a comrade, an ensign of our regiment. In those days though duels were severely punished, yet dueling was a kind of fashion among the officers — so strong and deeply rooted will a brutal prejudice sometimes be.

It was the end of June, and our meeting was to take place at seven o'clock the next day on the outskirts of the town — and then something happened that in very truth was the turning point of my life. Returning home in the evening, in a savage and brutal humor, I flew into a rage with Afanasy, my orderly, and gave him two blows in the face with all my might, so that it was covered with blood. He had not been long in my service, and I had struck him before but never with such ferocious cruelty. And believe me, though it's forty years ago, I recall it now with shame and pain. I went to bed and slept for about three hours; when I woke up the day was breaking. I got up — I did not want to sleep any more — I went to the window and opened it; it looked out upon the garden, I saw the sun rising, it was warm and beautiful, the birds were singing.

"What's the meaning of it," I thought, "the feeling in my heart as if there were something vile and shameful? Is it because I am going to shed blood? No, I feel it's not that. Can it be that I am afraid of death, afraid of being killed? No, that's not it, that's not it at all . . ." And all at once I knew what it was; it was because I had beaten Afanasy the evening before! It all rose before my mind, as if it were all repeated over again; he stood before me and I was beating him straight on the face, and he was holding his arms stiffly down, his head erect, his eyes fixed upon me as though on parade. He staggered at every blow and did not even dare to raise his hands to protect himself. That is what a man has been brought to; that was a man beating a fellowman! What a crime! It was as though a sharp dagger had pierced me right through. I stood as if I were struck dumb, while the sun was shining, the leaves were rejoicing, and the birds were trilling the praise of God . . . I hid my face in my hands, fell on my bed, and broke into a storm of tears. And then I remembered my brother Markel and what he said on his deathbed to his servants: "My dear ones, why do you wait on me, why do you love me, am I worth your waiting on me?"

"Yes, am I worth it?" flashed through my mind. After all, what am I worth that another man, a fellowman made in the likeness and image of God, should serve me? For the first time in my life this question struck me to the core. He had said, "Mother, my little heart, in truth we are each responsible to all for all, it's only that men don't know this. If they knew it, the world would be a paradise at once."

"God, can that too be false?" I thought as I wept. "In truth, perhaps, I am more than all others responsible for all, a greater sinner than all men in the world. And all at once the whole truth in its full light appeared to me: what was I going to do? I was going to kill a good, clever, noble man, who had done me no wrong; and by depriving his wife of happiness for the rest of her life, I should be torturing and killing her too. I lay thus in my bed with my face in the pillow, heedless how the time was passing. Suddenly my second, the ensign, came in with the pistols to fetch me.

"Ah," said he, "it's a good thing you are up already, it's time we were off, come along!"

I did not know what to do and hurried to and fro undecided; we went out to the carriage, however.

"Wait here a minute," I said to him. "I'll be back directly, I have forgotten my purse."

And I ran back alone, straight to Afanasy's little room.

"Afanasy," I said, "I gave you two blows on the face yesterday, forgive me," I said.

He started as though he were frightened, and looked at me; and I saw that it was not enough, and on the spot, in my full officer's uniform, I dropped at his feet and bowed my head to the ground.

"Forgive me," I said.

Then he was completely aghast.

"Your honor . . . sir, what are you doing? Am I worth it?"

And he burst out crying as I had done before, hid his face in his hands, turned to the window and shook all over with his sobs. I flew out to my comrade and jumped into the carriage.

"Ready," I cried. "Have you ever seen a conqueror?" I asked him. "Here is one before you."

I was in ecstasy, laughing and talking all the way, I don't remember what about.

He looked at me. "Well, brother, you are a plucky fellow, you'll keep up the honor of the uniform, I can see."

So we reached the place and found them there, waiting for us. We were placed twelve paces apart; he had the first shot. I stood gaily, looking him full in the face; I did not twitch an eyelash, I looked lovingly at him, for I knew what I would do. His shot just grazed my cheek and ear.

"Thank God," I cried, "no man has been killed," and I seized my pistol, turned back, and flung it far away into the wood.

"That's the place for you," I cried.

I turned to my adversary.

"Forgive me, young fool that I am, sir," I said, "for my unprovoked insult to you and for forcing you to fire at me. I am ten times worse than you and more, maybe. Tell that to the person you hold dearest in the world."

I had no sooner said this than they all three shouted at me.

"Upon my word," cried my adversary, annoyed, "if you did not want to fight, why didn't you let me alone?"

"Yesterday I was a fool, today I know better," I answered him gaily.

"As to yesterday, I believe you, but as for today, it is difficult to agree with your opinion," said he.

"Bravo," I cried, clapping my hands, "I agree with you there too, I have deserved it!"

"Will you shoot, sir, or not?"

"No, I won't," I said. "If you like, fire at me again, but it would be better for you not to fire."

The seconds, especially mine, were shouting too: "Can you disgrace the regiment like this, facing your antagonist and begging his forgiveness! If I'd only known this!"

I stood facing them all, not laughing now.

"Gentlemen," I said, "is it really so wonderful in these days to find a man who can repent of his stupidity and publicly confess his wrongdoing?"

"But not in a duel," cried my second again.

"That's what's so strange," I said. "For I ought to have owned my fault as soon as I got here, before he had fired a shot, before leading him into a great and deadly sin; but we have made our life so grotesque that to act in that way would have been almost impossible, for only after I had faced his shot at the distance of twelve paces could my words have any significance for him, and if I had spoken before, he would have said, 'He is a coward, the sight of the pistols frightened him, no use to listen to him.' Gentlemen," I cried suddenly, speaking straight from my heart, "look around you at the gifts of God, the clear sky, the pure air, the tender grass, the birds; nature is beautiful and sinless, and we, only we, are sinful and foolish, and we don't understand that life is heaven, for we have only to understand that and it will at once be fulfilled in all its beauty, we shall embrace each other and weep."

I would have said more but I could not; my voice broke with the sweetness and youthful gladness of it, and there was such bliss in my heart as I had never known before in my life.

"All this is rational and edifying," said my antagonist, "and in any case you are an original person."

"You may laugh," I said to him, laughing too, "but afterwards you will approve of me."

"Oh, I am ready to approve of you now," said he; "let us shake hands, for I believe you are genuinely sincere."

"No," I said, "not now, later on when I have grown

worthier and deserve your esteem, then shake hands and you will do well.''

We went home, my second upbraiding me all the way, while I kissed him. All my comrades heard of the affair at once and gathered together to pass judgment on me the same day.

"He has disgraced the uniform," they said. "Let him resign his commission."

Some stood up for me: "He faced the shot," they said.

"Yes, but he was afraid of his other shot and begged for forgiveness."

"If he had been afraid of being shot, he would have shot his own pistol first before asking forgiveness, but he flung it loaded into the forest. No, there's something else in this, something original."

I enjoyed listening and looking at them. "My dear friends and comrades," said I, "don't worry about my resigning my commission, for I have done so already. I have sent in my papers this morning, and as soon as I get my discharge I shall go into a monastery — it's with that object that I am leaving the regiment."

When I had said this every one of them burst out laughing.

"You should have told us of that first, that explains everything, we can't judge a monk."

They laughed and could not stop themselves, not scornfully but kindly and merrily. They all felt friendly toward me at once, even those who had been sternest in their censure, and all the following month, before my discharge came, they could not make enough of me. "Ah, you monk," they would say. And each one said something kind to me; they began trying to dissuade me, even to pity me: "What are you doing to yourself?"

"No," they would say then, "he is a brave fellow; he faced fire and could have fired his own pistol too, but he had a dream the night before that he should become a monk, and that's why he did it.''

It was the same thing with the society of the town. Till then I had been kindly received but had not been the object of special attention, and now all came to know me at once and invited me; they laughed at me, but they loved me. I may mention that although everybody talked openly of our duel, the authorities took no notice of it, because my antagonist was a near relation of our general, and as there had been no bloodshed and no serious consequences and as I resigned my commission, they took it as a joke. And I began then to speak aloud and fearlessly, regardless of their laughter, for it was always kindly and not spiteful laughter. These conversations mostly took place in the evenings, in the company of ladies; women particularly liked listening to me then, and they made the men listen.

"But how can I possibly be responsible for all?" everyone would laugh in my face. "Can I, for instance, be responsible for you?"

"You may well not know it," I would answer, "since the whole world has long been going on a different line, since we consider the veriest lies as truth and demand the same lies from others. Here I have for once in my life acted sincerely and — well — you all look upon me as a madman. Though you are friendly to me, yet you see, you all laugh at me."

"But how can we help being friendly to you?" said my hostess, laughing. The room was full of people. All of a sudden the young lady rose on whose account the duel had been fought and whom only lately I had intended to be my future wife. I had not noticed her coming into the room. She got up, came to me, and held out her hand.

"Let me tell you," she said, "that I am the first not to laugh at you, but on the contrary I thank you with tears and express my respect for you and for your action then."

Her husband too came up, and then they all approached

me and almost kissed me. My heart was filled with joy, but my attention was especially caught by a middle-aged man who came up to me with the others. I knew him by name already, but had never made his acquaintance or exchanged a word with him till that evening.

THE MYSTERIOUS VISITOR

He had long been an official in the town in a prominent position; he was respected by all, rich, and with a reputation for benevolence. He subscribed considerable sums to the almshouse and the orphan asylum; he was very charitable in secret too, a fact which only became known after his death. He was a man of about fifty, almost stern in appearance and not much given to conversation. He had been married about ten years, and his wife, who was still young, had borne him three children. I was sitting alone in my room one evening when my door suddenly opened and this gentleman walked in.

I must mention, by the way, that I was no longer living in my former quarters. As soon as I resigned my commission, I took rooms with an old lady, the widow of a government clerk. My landlady's servant waited upon me, for I had moved into her rooms simply because on my return from the duel I had sent Afanasy back to the regiment, as I felt ashamed to look him in the face after my last interview with him. So prone is the man of the world to be ashamed of any righteous action.

"I have," said my visitor, "with great interest listened to you speaking in different houses the last few days, and I wanted at last to make your personal acquaintance so as to talk to you more intimately. Can you, dear sir, grant me this favor?"

"I can, with the greatest pleasure, and I shall look upon

it as an honor.'' I said this, though I felt almost dismayed, so greatly was I impressed from the first moment by the appearance of this man. For though other people had listened to me with interest and attention, no one had come to me before with such a serious, stern, and concentrated expression. And now he had come to see me in my rooms. He sat down.

"You are, I see, a man of great strength of character," he said, "as you have dared to serve the truth, even when by doing so you risked incurring the contempt of all."

"Your praise is perhaps excessive," I replied.

"No, it's not excessive," he answered. "Believe me, such a course of action is far more difficult than you think. It is that which has impressed me, and it is only on that account that I have come to you," he continued. "Tell me, please, that is if you are not annoyed by my unseemly curiosity, what your exact sensations were, if you can recall them, at the moment when you made up your mind to ask forgiveness at the duel. Do not think my request frivolous; on the contrary, in asking the question I have a secret motive of my own, which I will perhaps explain to you later on if it is God's will that we should become more intimately acquainted."

All the while he was speaking, I was looking him straight in the face, and I felt all at once a complete trust in him and great curiosity on my side also, for I felt that there was some strange secret in his soul.

"You ask what were my exact sensations at the moment when I asked my opponent's forgiveness," I answered. "But I had better tell you from the beginning what I have not yet told anyone else." And I described all that had passed between Afanasy and me and how I had bowed down to the ground at his feet. "From that you can see for yourself," I concluded, "that at the time of the duel it was easier for me, for I had made a beginning already at home, and when once I had started on the road, to go further along it was far from being difficult but became a source of joy and happiness.''

I liked the way he looked at me as he listened. ''All that,'' he said, ''is exceedingly interesting. I will come to see you again and again.''

And from that time forth he came to see me nearly every evening. And we should have become greater friends if only he had also talked of himself. But he scarcely ever said a word about himself yet continually asked me about myself. In spite of that I became very fond of him and spoke with perfect frankness to him about all my feelings; for, thought I, what need have I to know his secrets, since I can see without that that he is a good man. Moreover, though he is such a serious man and my senior, he comes to see a youngster like me and treats me as his equal. And I learned from him a great deal that was profitable, for he was a man of lofty mind.

''That life is heaven,'' he said to me suddenly, ''that I have long been thinking about.'' And all at once he added, ''Indeed, I think of nothing else.'' He looked at me and smiled. ''I am more convinced of it than you are. I will tell you later why.''

I listened to him and thought that he evidently wanted to tell me something.

''Heaven,'' he went on, ''lies hidden within all of us — here it lies hidden in me now, and if I will it, it will be revealed to me tomorrow and for all time.''

I looked at him; he was speaking with great emotion and gazing mysteriously at me, as if he were questioning me.

''And that we are all responsible to all for all, apart from our own sins — you were quite right in thinking that, and it is wonderful how you could comprehend it in all its significance at once. And in very truth, as soon as men understand that, the Kingdom of Heaven will be for them not a dream, but a living reality.''

"And when," I cried out to him bitterly, "when will that come to pass? and will it ever come to pass? Is it not simply a dream of ours?"

"What, you don't believe it!" he said. "You preach it and don't believe it yourself. Believe me, this dream, as you call it, will come to pass without doubt; it will come, but not now, for every process has its law. It's a spiritual, psychological process. To transform the world, to recreate it afresh, men must turn into another path psychologically. Until you have really become in actual fact a brother to everyone, brotherhood will not come to pass. No sort of scientific teaching, no kind of common interest, will ever teach men to share property and privileges with equal consideration for all. Everyone will think his share too small, and they will be always envying, complaining, and attacking one another. You ask when it will come to pass; it will come to pass, but first we have to go through the period of isolation."

"What do you mean by isolation?" I asked him.

"Why, the isolation that prevails everywhere — above all in our age — yet has not fully developed; it has not reached its limit. For everyone strives to keep his individuality as apart as possible, wishes to secure the greatest possible fullness of life for himself; but meantime all his efforts result not in attaining fullness of life but in self-destruction, for instead of self-realization he ends by arriving at complete solitude. In our age all of mankind has split up into units; they all keep apart, each in his own groove; each one holds aloof from the rest, hides himself, and hides what he has. He ends by being repelled by others and repelling them. He heaps up riches by himself and thinks, 'How strong I am now and how secure,' and in his madness he does not understand that the more he heaps up, the more he sinks into self-destructive impotence. For he is accustomed to rely upon himself alone and to cut himself off from the whole; he has trained himself not to believe in the help of others, in men and in humanity, and only trembles for fear he should lose his money and the privileges that he has won for himself. Everywhere in these days men have, in their mockery, ceased to understand that the true security is to be found in social solidarity rather than in isolated individual effort. But this terrible individualism must inevitably have an end, and all will suddenly understand how unnaturally they have separated themselves from one another. It will be the spirit of the time, and people will marvel that they have sat so long in darkness without seeing the light. And then the sign of the Son of Man will be seen in the heavens . . . But until then we must keep the banner flying. Sometimes, even if he has to do it alone and his conduct seems to be crazy, a man must set an example and so draw men's souls out of their solitude and spur them to some act of brotherly love, so that the great idea may not die.''

Our evenings, one after another, were spent in such stirring and fervent talk. I gave up society and visited my neighbors much less frequently. Besides, I was no longer in fashion. I say this not as blame, for they still loved me and treated me good humoredly, but there's no denying that fashion is a great power in society. I began to regard my mysterious visitor with admiration, for besides enjoying his intelligence, I began to perceive that he was brooding over some plan in his heart and was preparing himself perhaps for a great step. Perhaps he liked my showing neither curiosity about his secret nor seeking to discover it by direct question or insinuation. But I noticed at last that he seemed to show signs of wanting to tell me something. This had become quite evident about a month after he first began to visit me.

"Do you know," he said once, "that people are very inquisitive about us in the town and wonder why I come to see you so often. But let them wonder, for *soon all will be explained.*"

Sometimes an extraordinary agitation would come over him, and almost always on such occasions he would get up and go away. Sometimes he would fix a long piercing look upon me, and I thought, "Now he will say something." But he would suddenly begin talking of something ordinary and familiar.

He often complained of headaches too.

One day, quite unexpectedly, after he had been talking with great fervor a long time, I saw him suddenly turn pale, and his face worked convulsively while he stared persistently at me.

"What's the matter?" I said; "do you feel ill?" — he had just been complaining of headache.

"I . . . do you know . . . I murdered someone."

He said this and smiled with a face as white as chalk. "Why is it he is smiling?" The thought flashed through my mind before I realized anything else. I too turned pale.

"What are you saying?" I cried.

"You see," he said with a pale smile, "how much it has cost me to say the first word. Now that I have said it, I feel I've taken the first step, and I shall go on."

For a long while I could not believe him, and I did not believe him at that time but only after he had been to see me three days running and told me all about it. At first I thought he was mad, but I ended by being convinced, to my great grief and amazement. His crime was a great and terrible one.

Fourteen years before, he had murdered the widow of a landowner, a wealthy and handsome young woman who had a house in our town. He had fallen passionately in love with her, declared his feeling, and tried to persuade her to marry him. But she had already given her heart to another man, an officer of noble birth and high rank in the service, who was at that time away at the front, though she was expecting him soon to return. She refused his offer and begged him not to come and see her. After he had ceased to visit her, he took advantage of his knowledge of the house to enter at night through the garden by the roof, at great risk of discovery. But as often happens, a crime committed with extraordinary audacity is more successful than others.

Entering the garret through the skylight, he went down the ladder, knowing that the door at the bottom of it was sometimes, through the negligence of the servants, left unlocked. He hoped to find it so, and so it was. He made his way in the dark to her bedroom, where a light was burning. As though on purpose, both her maids had gone off to a birthday party in the same street, without asking leave. The other servants slept in the servants' quarters or in the kitchen on the ground floor. His passion flamed up at the sight of her asleep, and then vindictive, jealous anger took possession of his heart, and beside himself, like a drunken man, he thrust a knife into her heart, so that she did not even cry out. Then with devilish and criminal cunning he contrived that suspicion should fall on the servants. He was so base as to take her purse, to open her chest with keys from under her pillow, and to take some things from it, doing it all as it might have been done by an ignorant servant, leaving valuable papers and taking only money. He took some of the larger gold things, but left smaller articles that were ten times as valuable. He took with him, too, some things for himself as remembrances, but of that later. Having done this awful deed, he returned by the way he had come.

Neither the next day, when the alarm was raised, nor at any time after in his life, did any one dream of suspecting that he was the criminal. In fact, no one knew of his love for her, for he was always reserved and silent and had no friend to whom he would have opened his heart. He was looked upon simply as an acquaintance, and not a very intimate one, of the murdered woman, since for the previous fortnight he had not even visited her. A serf of hers called Pyotr was at once suspected, and every circumstance confirmed the suspicion. The man knew — indeed his mistress did not conceal the fact — that having to send one of her serfs as a recruit, she had decided to send him, as he had no relations and his conduct was unsatisfactory. People had heard him angrily threatening to murder her when he was drunk in a tavern. Two days before her death, he had run away, staying no one knew where in the town. The day after the murder, he was found on the road leading out of the town, dead drunk, with a knife in his pocket and his right hand stained with blood for some reason. He declared that his nose had been bleeding, but no one believed him. The maids confessed that they had gone to a party and that the street door had been left open till they returned. And a number of similar details came to light, throwing suspicion on the innocent servant.

They arrested him, and he was tried for the murder; but a week after the arrest, the prisoner fell sick of a fever and died in the hospital while unconscious. There the matter ended, and the judges and the authorities and everyone in the town remained convinced that the crime had been committed by no one but the servant who had died in the hospital. And after that the punishment began.

My mysterious visitor, now my friend, told me that at first he was not in the least troubled by pangs of conscience. He was miserable a long time, but not for that reason; only from regret that he had killed the woman he loved, that she was no more, that in killing her he had killed his love, while the fire of passion was still in his veins. But of the innocent blood he had shed, of the murder of a fellow human, he scarcely thought. The thought that his victim might have become the wife of another man was unendurable to him, and so for a long time he was convinced in his conscience that he could not have acted otherwise.

At first he was worried at the arrest of the servant, but his illness and death soon set his mind at rest, for the man's death was apparently (so he reflected at the time) not owing to his arrest or his fright but to a chill he had taken on the day he ran away, when he had lain all night dead drunk on the damp ground. The theft of the money and other things troubled him little, for he argued that the theft had not been committed for gain but to avert suspicion. The sum stolen was small, and he shortly afterwards subscribed the whole of it, and much more, towards the funds for maintaining an almshouse in the town. He did this on purpose to set his conscience at rest about the theft, and it's a remarkable fact that for a long time he really was at peace — he told me this himself. He entered then upon a career of great activity in the service, volunteered for a difficult and arduous duty, which occupied him two years, and being a man of strong will almost forgot the past. Whenever he recalled it, he tried not to think of it at all. He became active in philanthropy too, founded and helped to maintain many institutions in the town, did a good deal in the two capitals, and was elected a member of philanthropic societies in both Moscow and Petersburg.

At last, however, he began brooding over the past, and the strain of it was too much for him. Then he was attracted by a fine and intelligent girl and soon after married her, hoping that marriage would dispel his lonely depression and that by entering on a new life and scrupulously doing his duty to his wife and children, he would escape from old memories altogether. But the very opposite of what he expected happened. He began, even in the first month of his marriage, to be continually fretted by the thought, "My wife loves me — but what if she knew?" When she first told him that she would soon bear him a child, he was troubled. "I am giving life, but I have taken life." Children came. "How dare I love them, teach and educate them; how can I talk to them of virtue? I have shed blood." They were splendid children, and he longed to caress them: "But I can't look at their fair and innocent faces, I am unworthy."

At last he began to be bitterly and ominously haunted by the blood of his murdered victim, by the young life he had destroyed, by the blood that cried out for vengeance. He began to have terrible dreams. But being a man of fortitude, he bore his suffering a long time, thinking, "I shall expiate everything by this secret agony." But that hope too was vain; the longer it went on, the more intense was his suffering.

He was respected in society for his active benevolence, though everyone was overawed by his stern and gloomy character. But the more he was respected, the more intolerable it was for him. He confessed to me that he had thoughts of killing himself. But he began to be haunted by another idea — an idea which he had at first regarded as impossible and unthinkable, though at last it got such a hold on his heart that he could not shake it off. He dreamed of rising up, going out, and confessing in the face of all men that he had committed murder. For three years this dream had pursued him, haunting him in different forms. At last he believed with his whole heart that if he confessed his crime, he would heal his soul and be at peace forever. But this belief filled his heart with terror, for how could he carry it out? And then came the occurrence of my duel.

"Looking at you, I have made up my mind."

I looked at him.

"Is it possible," I cried, clasping my hands, "that such a trivial incident could give rise to such a resolution in you?"

"My resolution has been growing for the last three years," he answered, "and your story only gave the last touch to it. Looking at you, I reproached myself and envied you," he said to me almost harshly.

"But you won't be believed," I observed; "it's fourteen years ago."

"I have proofs, great proofs, I shall show them."

Then I cried and kissed him.

"Tell me one thing, one thing," he said (as though it all

depended upon me), "my wife, my children! My wife may die of grief, and though my children won't lose their rank and property, they'll be a convict's children — forever! And what a memory, what a memory of me I shall leave in their hearts!"

I said nothing.

"And to part from them, to leave them forever? It's forever, you know, forever!"

I sat still and repeated a silent prayer. I got up at last. I felt afraid.

"Well?" He looked at me.

"Go!" said I, "Confess. Everything passes, only the truth remains. Your children will understand when they grow up, the nobility of your resolution."

He left me that time as though he had made up his mind. Yet for more than a fortnight afterward, he came to me every evening still preparing himself, still unable to bring himself to the point. He made my heart ache. One day he would come determined and say fervently:

"I know it will be heaven for me, heaven, the moment I confess. Fourteen years I've been in hell. I want to suffer. I will take my punishment and begin to live. You can pass through the world doing wrong, but there's no turning back. Now I dare not love my neighbor nor even my own children. Good God, my children will understand, perhaps, what my punishment has cost me and will not condemn me! God is not in strength but in truth."

"All will understand your sacrifice," I said to him, "if not at once, they will understand later; for you have served truth, the higher truth, not of the earth."

And he would go away seeming comforted, but next day he would come again, bitter, pale, sarcastic.

"Every time I come to you, you look at me so inquisitively as though to say, 'He has still not confessed!' Wait a bit longer — don't despise me too much. It's not such an easy thing to do as you think. Perhaps I shall not do it at all. You won't go and inform against me then, will you?''

And far from looking at him with indiscreet curiosity, I was afraid to look at him at all. I was quite ill from anxiety, and my heart was full of tears. I could not sleep at night.

"I have just come from my wife," he went on. "Do you you understand what the word 'wife' means? When I went out the children called to me, 'Good–bye, Father, come back quickly to read *The Children's Magazine* with us.' No, you don't understand that! No one is wise from another man's woe.''

His eyes were glittering, his lips were twitching. Suddenly he struck the table with his fist so that everything on it danced — it was the first time he had done such a thing; he was such a mild man.

"But need I?" he exclaimed, "must I? No one has been condemned, no one has been sent to Siberia in my place, the man died of fever. And I've been punished by my sufferings for the blood I shed. And I shan't be believed; they won't believe my proofs. Need I confess, need I? I am ready to go on suffering all my life for the blood I have shed if only my wife and children may be spared. Will it be justice to ruin them along with myself? Aren't we making a mistake? What is right in this case? And will people recognize it, will they appreciate it, will they respect it?''

"Good Lord!" I thought to myself, "he is thinking of other people's respect at such a moment!" And I felt so sorry for him then, that I believe I would have shared his fate if it could have comforted him. I saw he was beside himself. I was aghast, realizing with my heart as well as my mind what such a resolution meant.

"Decide my fate!" he exclaimed again.

"Go and confess," I whispered to him. My voice failed me, but I whispered it firmly. I took up the New Testament from the table, the Russian translation, and showed him the Gospel of St. John, Chapter 12, Verse 24:

"Verily, verily, I say unto you, except a corn of wheat fall into the ground and die, it abideth alone: but if it die, it bringeth forth much fruit."

I had just been reading that verse when he came in. He read it.

"That's true," he said, but he smiled bitterly. "It's terrible the things you find in those books," he said after a pause. "It's easy enough to thrust them upon one. And who wrote them? Can they have been written by men?"

"The Holy Spirit wrote them," said I.

"It's easy for you to prate," he smiled again, this time almost with hatred.

I took the book again, opened it in another place and showed him the Epistle to the Hebrews, Chapter 10, Verse 31. He read:

"It is a fearful thing to fall into the hands of the living God."

He read it and simply flung down the book. He was trembling all over.

"An awful text," he said. "There's no denying you've picked out fitting ones." He rose from the chair. "Well!" he said, "good-bye, perhaps I shan't come again . . . we shall meet in heaven. So I have been fourteen years 'in the hands of the living God.' That's how one must think of those fourteen years. Tomorrow I will beseech those hands to let me go."

I wanted to take him in my arms and kiss him, but I did not dare — his face was contorted and sombre. He went away.

"Good God," I thought, "what has he gone to face!" I fell on my knees before the ikon and wept for him before the Holy Mother of God, our swift defender and helper. I was half an hour praying in tears, and it was late, about midnight. Suddenly I saw the door open and he came in again. I was surprised.

"Where have you been?" I asked him.

"I think," he said, "I've forgotten something . . . my handkerchief, I think . . . Well, even if I've not forgotten anything, let me stay a little."

He sat down. I stood over him.

"You sit down, too," said he.

I sat down. We sat still for two minutes; he looked intently at me and suddenly smiled — I remembered that — then he got up, embraced me warmly, and kissed me.

"Remember," he said, "how I came to you a second time. Do you hear? Remember it!"

And he went out.

"Tomorrow," I thought.

And so it was. I did not know that evening that the next day was his birthday. I had not been out for the last few days so I had no chance of hearing it from anyone. On that day he always had a great gathering; everyone in the town went to it. It was the same this time. After dinner he walked into the middle of the room with a paper in his hand — a formal declaration to the chief of his department who was present. This declaration he read aloud to the whole assembly. It contained a full account of the crime, in every detail.

"I cut myself off from men as a monster. God has visited me," he said in conclusion. "I want to suffer for my sin!"

Then he brought out and laid on the table all the things he had been keeping for fourteen years that he thought would prove his crime: the jewels belonging to the murdered woman that he had stolen to divert suspicion; a cross and a locket taken from her neck with a portrait of her betrothed in the locket; her notebook and two letters, one from her betrothed telling her that he would soon be with her, and her unfinished answer left on the table to be sent off next day. He had carried off these two letters — what for? Why had he kept them for fourteen years instead of destroying them as evidence against him?

And this is what happened: everyone was amazed and horrified, everyone refused to believe it and thought that he was deranged, though all listened with intense curiosity. A few days later it was fully decided and agreed in every house that the unhappy man was mad. The legal authorities could not refuse to take the case up, but they too dropped it. Though the trinkets and letters made them ponder, they decided that even if they did turn out to be authentic, no charge could be based on those alone. Besides, she might have given him those things as a friend or asked him to take care of them for her. I heard afterwards, however, that the genuineness of the things was proved by the friends and relations of the murdered woman and that there was no doubt about them. Yet nothing was destined to come of it, after all.

Five days later all had heard that he was ill and that his life was in danger. The nature of his illness I can't explain; they said it was a malady of the heart. But it became known that the doctors had been induced by his wife to investigate his mental condition also and had come to the conclusion that it was a case of insanity. I betrayed nothing, though people ran to question me. But when I wanted to visit him, I was for a long while forbidden to do so, above all by his wife.

"It's you who have caused his illness," she said to me; "he was always gloomy, but for the last year people noticed that he was peculiarly excited and did strange things, and now you have been the ruin of him. Your preaching has brought him to this; for the last month he was always with you."

Indeed, not only his wife but the whole town were down upon me and blamed me. "It's all your doing," they said. I was silent but rejoiced at heart, for I saw plainly God's mercy to the man who had turned against himself and punished himself. I could not believe in his insanity.

They let me see him at last; he insisted upon saying good-bye to me. I went in to him and saw at once that not only his days but his hours were numbered. He was weak and yellow, his hands trembled, and he gasped for breath, but his face was full of tender and happy feeling.

"It is done!" he said. "I've long been yearning to see you; why didn't you come?"

I did not tell him that they would not let me see him.

"God has had pity on me and is calling me to Himself. I know I am dying, but I feel joy and peace for the first time after so many years. There was heaven in my heart from the moment I had done what I had to do. Now I dare to love my children and to kiss them. Neither my wife nor the judges nor anyone else has believed it. My children will never believe it either. I see in that God's mercy to them. I shall die, and my name will be without a stain for them. And now I feel God near, my heart rejoices as in Heaven . . . I have done my duty."

He could not speak, he gasped for breath, he pressed my hand warmly, looking fervently at me. We did not talk for long; his wife kept peeping in at us. But he had time to whisper to me:

"Do you remember how I came back to you that second time at midnight? I told you to remember it. You know what I came back for? I came to kill you!"

I started.

"I went out from you then into the darkness; I wandered about the streets, struggling with myself. And suddenly I hated you so that I could hardly bear it. Now, I thought, he is all that binds me, and he is my judge. I can't refuse to face my punishment tomorrow, for he knows all. It was not that I was afraid you would betray me (I never even thought of that) but I thought, 'How can I look him in the face if I don't confess?' And if you had been at the other end of the earth, but alive, it would have been all the same; the thought was unendurable that you were alive, knowing everything and condemning me.

I hated you as though you were the cause, as though you were to blame for everything. I came back to you then, remembering that you had a dagger lying on your table. I sat down and asked you to sit down, and for a whole minute I pondered. If I had killed you, I should have been ruined by that murder even if I had not confessed the other. But I didn't think about that at all, and I didn't want to think of it at that moment. I only hated you and longed to revenge myself on you for everything. The Lord vanquished the devil in my heart. But let me tell you, you were never nearer death.''

A week later he died. The whole town followed him to the grave. The chief priest made a speech full of feeling. All lamented the terrible illness that had cut short his days. But all the town was up in arms against me after the funeral, and people even refused to see me. Some, at first a few and afterwards more, began to believe in the truth of his story, and they visited me and questioned me with great interest and eagerness, for man loves to see the downfall and disgrace of the righteous. But I held my tongue, and very shortly after, I left the town, and five months later by God's grace I entered upon the safe and blessed path, praising the unseen finger which had guided me so clearly to it. But I remember in my prayer to this day the servant of God, Mihail, who suffered so greatly.

The Wedding at Cana

Alyosha Karamazov had experienced a deep shock. The body of his starets or elder, Zossima, whom he had loved above all, had not resisted corruption after death in an odor of sanctity, as was definitely expected and had been observed in the case of almost all the others who had died like him. On the contrary, very soon after his death a pronounced smell of death had come from his body, very much to the malicious pleasure of the many monks who had opposed and envied Zossima. This had made such an impression on Alyosha that suddenly nothing on this earth mattered to him anymore, and he allowed Rakitin to take him along to see Grushenka. (The relationships of these three characters is told more fully in the introductory paragraphs on pages 155 and 142.) He withstood her efforts to seduce him, however, brought her to her senses, and returned, inwardly renewed, to the monastery where he took on the death watch with the dead man so beloved by him. Here begins his vision or dream.

It was very late, according to monastery order, when Alyosha returned to the hermitage; the door keeper let him in by a special entrance. It had struck nine o'clock — the hour of rest and repose after a day of such agitation for all. Alyosha timidly opened the door and went into the elder's cell where his coffin was now standing. There was no one in the cell but Father Païssy, reading the Gospel in solitude over the coffin, and the young novice Porfiry, exhausted by the previous night's conversation and the disturbing incidents of the day, was sleeping the deep, sound sleep of youth on the floor of the other room. Though Father Païssy heard Alyosha come in, he did not even look in his direction. Alyosha turned to the right from the door to the corner, fell on his knees, and began to pray.

His soul was overflowing but with mingled feelings; no single sensation stood out distinctly; on the contrary, one drove out another in a slow, continual rotation. But there was a sweetness in his heart and, strange to say, Alyosha was not surprised at it. Again he saw that coffin before him, the hidden, dead figure so precious to him, but the weeping and poignant grief of the morning was no longer aching in his soul. As soon as he came in, he fell down before the coffin as before a holy shrine; but joy, joy, was glowing in his mind and in his heart. The one window of the cell was open, the air was fresh and cool. "So the smell must have become stronger, if they opened the window," thought Alyosha. But even this thought of the smell of corruption, which had seemed to him so awful and humiliating a few hours before, no longer made him feel miserable or indignant. He began praying quietly, but he soon felt that he was praying almost mechanically. Fragments of thought floated through his soul, flashed like stars, and went out again at once, to be succeeded by others. Yet there was reigning in his soul a sense of the wholeness of things — something steadfast and comforting — and he was aware of it himself. Sometimes he began praying ardently; he longed to pour out his thankfulness and love . . .

But when he had begun to pray, he passed suddenly to something else and sank into thought, forgetting both the prayer and what had interrupted it. He began listening to what Father Païssy was reading, but worn out with exhaustion he gradually began to doze.

"And the third day there was a marriage in Cana of Galilee;" read Father Païssy. *"And the mother of Jesus was*

there; and both Jesus was called, and his disciples, to the marriage.''

''Marriage? What's that . . . A marriage!'' floated whirling through Alyosha's mind. ''There is happiness for her, too . . . She has gone to the feast . . . No, she has not taken the knife . . . That was only a tragic phrase . . . Well . . . tragic phrases should be forgiven, they must be. Tragic phrases comfort the heart . . . without them, sorrow would be too heavy for men to bear. Rakitin has gone off to the back-alley. As long as Rakitin broods over his wrongs, he will always go off to the back-alley . . . But the high road . . . the road is wide and straight and bright as crystal, and the sun is at the end of it . . . Oh, what's being read? . . .''

''And when they wanted wine, the mother of Jesus saith unto him; 'They have no wine' . . .'' Alyosha heard.

''Ah, yes, I was missing that, and I didn't want to miss it, I love that passage; it's Cana of Galilee, the first miracle . . . Ah, that miracle! Ah, that sweet miracle! It was not men's grief but their joy Christ visited; He worked His first miracle to help men's gladness . . . 'He who loves men loves their gladness, too . . .' *he* was always repeating that, it was one of his leading ideas . . . 'There's no living without joy,' Mitya says . . . Yes, Mitya . . . 'Everything that is true and good is always full of forgiveness,' he used to say that, too . . .''

''Jesus saith unto her, Woman, what has it to do with thee or me? Mine hour is not yet come.

''His mother saith unto the servants: Whatsoever he saith unto you, do it . . .''

''Do it . . . Gladness, the gladness of some poor, very poor, people . . . Of course they were poor, since they hadn't wine enough even at a wedding . . . The historians write that in those days the people living about the Lake of Gennesaret were the poorest that can possibly be imagined . . . and another great heart, that other great being, His mother, knew that He had come not only to make His great terrible sacrifice. She knew that His heart was open even to the simple, artless merrymaking of some obscure and unlearned people, who had warmly bidden Him to their poor wedding. 'Mine hour is not yet come,' He said, with a soft smile. (He must have smiled gently to her.) And indeed was it to make wine abundant at poor weddings He had come down to earth? And yet He went and did as she asked Him . . . Ah, he is reading again . . ."

"*Jesus saith unto them, Fill the waterpots with water. And they filled them up to the brim.*

"*And he saith unto them, Draw out now and bear unto the governor of the feast. And they bare it.*

"*When the ruler of the feast had tasted the water that was made wine and knew not whence it was (but the servants which drew the water knew), the governor of the feast called the bridegroom,*

"*And saith unto him: Every man at the beginning doth set forth good wine; and when men have well drunk, that which is worse; but thou hast kept the good wine until now.*"

"But what's this, what's this? Why is the room growing wider? . . . Ah, yes . . . It's the marriage, the wedding . . . yes, of course. Here are the guests, here is the young couple sitting, and the merry crowd and . . . Where is the wise governor of the feast? But who is this? Who? Again the walls are receding . . . Who is getting up there from the great table? What! . . . He here, too? But he's in the coffin . . . but he's here, too. He has stood up, he sees me, he is coming here . . . Oh, God!"

Yes, he went up to him — to him — he, the little, thin old man, with tiny wrinkles on his face, joyful and laughing softly. There was no coffin now, and he was in the same dress as he had worn yesterday sitting with them, when the visitors had gathered about him. His face was uncovered, his eyes

were shining. How was this then, he too had been called to the feast. He too at the marriage of Cana in Galilee . . .

"Yes, my dear, I am called too, called and bidden," he heard a soft voice saying over him. "Why have you hidden yourself here, out of sight? You come and join us too."

It was his voice, the voice of Father Zossima. And it must be he, since he called him!

The elder raised Alyosha by the hand, and he rose from his knees.

"We are rejoicing," the little, thin old man went on. "We are drinking the new wine, the wine of new, great gladness; do you see how many guests? Here are the bride and bridegroom, here is the wise governor of the feast, he is tasting the new wine. Why do you wonder at me? I gave an onion to a beggar, so I too am here. And many here have given only an onion each — only one little onion . . . What are all our deeds? And you, my gentle one, you, my kind boy, you too have known how to give a famished woman an onion today. Begin your work, dear one, begin it, gentle one! . . . Do you see our Sun, do you see Him?"

"I am afraid . . . I dare not look," whispered Alyosha.

"Do not fear Him. He is terrible in His greatness, awful in His sublimity, but infinitely merciful. He has made Himself like unto us from love and rejoices with us. He is changing the water into wine so that the gladness of the guests may not be cut short. He is expecting new guests; He is calling new ones unceasingly for ever and ever . . . There they are bringing new wine. Do you see they are bringing the vessels . . ."

Something glowed in Alyosha's heart, something filled it till it ached, tears of rapture rose from his soul . . . He stretched out his hands, uttered a cry and awoke.

Again the coffin, the open window, and the soft, solemn, distinct reading of the Gospel. But Alyosha did not listen to the reading. It was strange, he had fallen asleep on his knees, but now he was on his feet, and suddenly, as though thrown forward, with three firm rapid steps he went right up to the coffin. His shoulder brushed against Father Païssy without his noticing it. Father Païssy raised his eyes for an instant from his book, but looked away again at once, seeing that something strange was happening to the boy. Alyosha gazed for half a minute at the coffin, at the covered, motionless dead man that lay in the coffin, with the ikon on his breast and the peaked cap with the octangular cross on his head. He had only just been hearing his voice, and that voice was still ringing in his ears. He was listening, still expecting other words, but suddenly he turned sharply and went out of the cell.

He did not stop on the steps either, but went quickly down; his soul, overflowing with rapture, yearned for freedom, space, openness. The vault of heaven, full of soft, shining stars, stretched vast and fathomless above him. The Milky Way ran in two pale streams from the zenith to the horizon. The fresh, motionless, still night enfolded the earth. The white towers and golden domes of the cathedral gleamed out against the sapphire sky. The gorgeous autumn flowers in the beds round the house were slumbering till morning. The silence of earth seemed to melt into the silence of the heavens. The mystery of earth was one with the mystery of the stars.

Alyosha stood, gazed, and suddenly threw himself down on the earth. He did not know why he embraced it. He could not have told why he longed so irresistibly to kiss it, to kiss it all. But he kissed it weeping, sobbing, and watering it with his tears and vowed passionately to love it, to love it for ever and ever. "Water the earth with the tears of your joy and love those tears," echoed in his soul.

What was he weeping over?

Oh! in his rapture he was weeping even over those stars, which were shining at him from the abyss of space, and "he was not ashamed of that ecstasy." There seemed to be threads from all those innumerable worlds of God, linking his soul to them, and it was trembling all over "in contact with other worlds." He longed to forgive everyone for everything, and to beg forgiveness — oh not for himself but for all men, for all and for everything. "And others are praying for me too," echoed again in his soul. But with every instant he felt clearly and, as it were, tangibly, that something firm and unshakable as that vault of heaven had entered into his soul. It was as though some idea had seized the sovereignty of his mind — and it was for all his life and for ever and ever. He had fallen on the earth a weak boy, but he rose up a resolute champion, and he knew and felt it suddenly at the very moment of his ecstasy. And never, never, all his life long, could Alyosha forget that minute.

"Someone visited my soul in that hour," he used to say afterwards, with implicit faith in his words.

Within three days he left the monastery in accordance with the words of his elder, who had bidden him "sojourn in the world."

LIFE IN GOD

Talks With an Old Friend of God

This passage is taken from The Adolescent (A Raw Youth), *Dostoyevsky's too little esteemed psychological novel, which he wrote immediately before his last work,* The Brothers Karamazov. *Makar Evanovich Dolgoruky is a former serf and the legal husband of the mother of the "adolescent," the illegitimate son of the onetime landowner Versilov, who is also spoken of here. Arkady Dolgoruky, "the adolescent," is narrator in this exchange with Makar.*

"Ah, it's bad to be old and sick," he sighed. "One wonders why the soul should hang on like that in the body and still enjoy being alive. It seems that, if I were given a chance to start my life all over again, my soul wouldn't mind at all, although I guess that's a sinful thought."

"Why sinful?"

"Because it's a wish, a dream, while an old man should leave life gracefully. Murmuring and protesting when one meets death is a great sin. But I guess God would forgive even an old man if he got to love life out of the gaiety of his soul. It's hard for a man to know what's sinful and what's not, for there's a mystery in it that's beyond human ken. So a pious old man must be content at all times and must die in the full light of understanding, blissfully and gracefully, satisfied with the days that have been given him to live, yearning for his last hour, and rejoicing when he is gathered like a stalk of wheat unto the sheaf when he has fulfilled his mysterious destiny."

"You keep talking about 'mystery'? What does it mean 'fulfilling one's mysterious destiny'?" I asked, looking around toward the door.

I was glad we were alone and surrounded by complete stillness. The sun that had not set yet shone brightly in the window. He spoke somewhat grandiloquently and none too coherently, but with great sincerity and a strange excitement that suggested he was truly glad I was there with him. But I also noticed certain unmistakable signs that he was feverish, very feverish as a matter of fact. But I too was ill and had been feverish myself when I'd come to his room.

"What's mystery? Everything's mystery, my friend, everything is God's mystery. There's mystery in every tree, in every blade of grass. When a little bird sings or all those many, many stars shine in the sky at night — it's all mystery, the same one. But the greatest mystery is what awaits man's soul in the world beyond, and that's the truth, my boy."

"I don't quite see what you mean . . . Believe me, I'm not trying to tease you and, I assure you, I do believe in God. But all these mysteries you're talking about have been solved by human intelligence long ago, and whatever hasn't yet been completely solved will be, and perhaps very soon. The botanist today knows perfectly well how a tree grows, and the physiologist and the anatomist know perfectly well what makes a bird sing; or at least they'll know it very soon . . . As to the stars, not only have they all been counted, but all their movements have been calculated with an accuracy down to the last second, so that it's possible to predict, say a thousand years ahead, the exact day and time of the appearance of a comet. And now even the chemical composition of the most remote stars has become known to us . . . Also, take for instance a microscope, which is a sort of glass that can magnify things a million times, and look at a drop of water through it. You'll see a whole new world full of unseen living creatures. Well, that too was a mystery once, but science has now explained it.''

"I've heard about all that, my boy; people have told me many times about these things. And this is certainly great and glorious knowledge. Whatever man has, has been given him by God, and with good reason it was said that the Lord did breathe into man the breath of life to live and learn.''

"Of course, of course, but those are just commonplaces. You're not really an enemy of science, are you? You wouldn't be some sort of partisan of a state under church control or . . . But I don't suppose you'd understand . . .''

"No, my friend, you've got me wrong; I've always respected science since I was a boy and, although I can't understand it myself, that's all right: science may be beyond my ken, but it is within the ken of other men. And it's best that way because then everyone has what comes to him, and not everyone is made to understand science. Otherwise every man thinks he can do everything and wants to astonish the whole world, and I'd be the worst of them all perhaps if I had the skill to do it. But since I don't have those skills, how can I hold forth before others, ignorant as I am? But you're young and clever and, since you've been given these advantages, go ahead and study. Get to know everything so that if you meet a godless man or a man with evil intentions, you can answer him properly, and his wicked and impious words will not befog your young mind . . . As to that glass you mentioned, I've seen it; in fact, the last time was not so very long ago . . .''

He took a deep breath and sighed. No doubt about it: he was enjoying talking to me very much indeed. He was very anxious to communicate. Moreover, I'm sure I'm not just imagining things if I say that at certain moments he looked at me with a strange, even uncanny love, as his hand came to rest tenderly on top of mine or as he gently patted my shoulder. I must say, however, that at other moments he seemed to forget altogether that I was there, but he went on talking just as eagerly, and I could imagine him sitting all alone in the room and addressing the walls.

"I know a man of great wisdom who's now living in the Gennadieva Desert," he went on, "a man of noble birth who was rich and was also a lieutenant colonel in the cavalry. He couldn't face the bonds of marriage and withdrew from the world to seek silent and solitary retreats where he felt sheltered from worldly vanities. And so he's lived — it's almost ten years now — a life of great austerity, practicing the renunciation of all earthly desires, but he still refuses to take monastic vows . . . Now it so happens that Peter Valerianovich — that's his name — has more books than I've ever seen in any one man's possession; in fact, he has eight thousand rubles' worth of books — he told me so himself; and I've learned many things from him on various occasions, for I've always loved to listen to him talk. Well, one day I asked him, 'How is it, sir, that a man as learned and intelligent as you, who has spent almost ten years living like a monk, who has learned to control his will and has renounced all earthly desires, how is it that you still refuse to take proper monastic vows and so become even more perfect?' 'You just said something about my being so learned and intelligent, old man,' he said to me; 'well, that learning and intelligence may be my trouble; they're still holding me in bondage instead of my controlling them. As to living like a monk, it may just have become an old habit with me and I'm not even aware of it. And when it comes to my renunciation of worldly desires, let me tell you this: true, I thought nothing of signing away my estates or resigning my lieutenant colonel's commission . . . But, you know, for more than nine years now I've been trying to give up smoking my pipe and thus far I have failed. So what kind of monk would I make and how could I claim to have mastered my desires?'

"I marvelled at such a humility. And then, last summer

on St. Peter's day, I again found myself in that desert — God just willed it that way — and when I walked into his cell, I saw it standing there, that thing, the microscope; he had ordered it from abroad and paid a lot of money for it. 'Wait, old man,' he said to me, 'I'll show you something very strange, something that you've never seen before. Here, see this drop of water that looks as pure as a tear? All right then, look at it now and you'll see that scientists will soon explain all the mysteries of God without leaving a single one to you and me.' That was just how he put it and it stuck in my mind. But it so happened that I'd already looked into a microscope thirty-five years before that, Mr. Malgasov's microscope, my old master and Mr. Versilov's maternal uncle, one of whose estates he later inherited. Mr. Malgasov was a very important general and a big landowner, who kept a huge pack of hounds and whose huntsman I was for many years. When he brought home that microscope and installed it, Mr. Malgasov had all his serfs assembled — everybody, men and women — and ordered them to look into it in turn; they were shown one after another a louse, a flea, the point of a needle, a hair, and a drop of water. And it was very funny — they were afraid to look into the thing, but they were also afraid to incur Mr. Malgasov's anger, for he was pretty short-tempered, our master. Some of the serfs didn't know how to look into a microscope and they narrowed their eyes so much that they couldn't make out anything; others were so scared that they cried out from fright, while old Savin Makarov put both hands over his eyes and shouted: 'Do whatever you want to me, I won't come near it!' And there was a lot of stupid laughing. But I didn't tell Peter Valerianovich that I'd already had a glimpse into this wonder thirty-five years before, because I saw how much he was enjoying showing it to me and, indeed, I started marveling out loud and pretending to be horrified. He gave me time to recover and then asked: 'Well, what do you say to that, old man?' And I bowed down and answered him: 'The Lord said let there be light and there was light.' To that he answered: 'And shouldn't there be darkness too?' He said these words in such a strange way without even smiling that I was very surprised, but then he seemed annoyed at something and fell silent.''

"It all seems very plain to me," I said; "your Peter Valerianovich is eating his rice and raisins in his monastery and bowing to the ground while he doesn't really believe in God. And you simply stumbled upon him at just such a moment. Besides," I added, "he seems to be a rather peculiar man because surely he must have looked into his microscope at least ten times before, so why should the eleventh glimpse all but drive him out of his mind? It's some sort of nervousness or oversensitivity that he must have contracted living in the monastery . . ."

"He's a man with a pure heart and a high intelligence, and he's not an atheist," Makar said firmly. "His brain is astir with ideas and his heart is restless. There are many people like him nowadays among the gentry and among the learned ones. And let me tell you this: the man is punishing himself. You should leave such folks alone, not annoy them, they're worthy of respect, and you ought to mention them in your prayers before going to sleep because they're searching for God. You do pray before going to sleep, don't you?''

"No, I don't. I consider it an empty ritual. But I'll admit this much: I rather like your Peter Valerianovich. Whatever else he is, he's not one of those puppets but a real man who reminds me rather of someone whom we both know very well.''

The old man seemed to register only the first part of what I'd just said.

"It's a pity you don't pray, dear friend; a prayer gladdens the heart before you go to sleep in the evening, when you wake up in the morning, and if you awake in the night . . . Now let me tell you something else. Last summer, in July, many of us pilgrims were hurrying to the Monastery of Our Lady for the holy day. The closer we came to the place, the more there were of us, and finally we were almost two hundred, all going to kiss the holy and miraculous relics of the two great saints Aniky and Gregory. We spent the night, my friend, in an open field, and I awoke early in the morning when everyone else was still asleep and the sun hadn't even peeped out from behind the forest yet. I lifted my head, my boy, and looked around, and everything was so beautiful that it couldn't be put into words, so I just sighed. It was still and quiet, the air was light, and the grass was growing . . . Grow, God's grass, grow! . . . A bird sang . . . Sing, you little bird of God! . . . A little babe squeaked in a woman's arms . . . God bless you, little man, grow and be happy, dear child! . . . And for the first time in my life I became conscious of all that was going on inside me. I put my head down again and went back to sleep, and it was so nice. It's so good to be alive, my dear boy! If I should get better, I'll go wandering again come spring . . . And if there's mystery in the world, it only makes it even better; it fills the heart with awe and wonder, and it gladdens the heart: 'All is in you, oh Lord, and so am I, and so keep me . . .' Do not repine, boy, mystery makes it even more beautiful,'' he added with tender fervor.

"You mean it's even more beautiful because there's mystery in it. I'll remember that. You express yourself very clumsily, but I understand what you mean; I feel that you know and understand much more than you can put into words . . . Still you sound as if you were feverish . . .''

This last remark slipped from my lips inadvertently as I stared at his shining eyes and his face, which had grown even paler.

But I don't believe he heard me.

"You know, my boy," he said, as if pursuing a thought that had been interrupted, "there's a limit to how long a man is remembered on this earth. It's about a hundred years, that limit. Less than a hundred years after a man's death he may still be remembered by his children or perhaps his grandchildren who have seen his face, but after that time, even if his name is still remembered, it's only indirectly, from other people's words, and it's just an idea about him, because all those who have seen him alive will by then be dead too. And grass will grow over his grave in the cemetery, the white stone over him will crumble, and everyone will forget him, including his own descendants, because only very few names remain in people's memory. So that's all right — let them forget! yes, go on, forget me, dear ones, but me, I'll go on loving you even from my grave. I can hear, dear children, your cheerful voices and I can hear your steps on the graves of your fathers; live for some time yet in the sunlight and enjoy yourselves while I pray for you and I'll come to you in your dreams . . . Death doesn't make any difference, for there's love after death too!"

"You see, I used to be terribly afraid at first of those learned people, of those professors," Makar, who must have said something about professors before, went on, with his eyes slightly lowered. "Ah, the way they used to scare me! I didn't dare say anthing to them because there was nothing I was more afraid of than an atheist. I have only one soul, I used to say to myself, and if I lose it, I'll never find another. But later I was no longer afraid of them. Why, I thought, they're not gods after all, they're simply men with all the human weaknesses, just like us. And I was curious too: I wanted to know what that godlessness of theirs was really like. After a time, though, even that curiosity passed."

He stopped, although he seemed to want to go on talking; the same serene smile still played on his lips.

There are simple and unaffected souls who trust everybody and are not aware of the ridiculous. Such people are of limited intelligence because they're eager to reveal to any comer their most sacred secrets. But I felt there was something other than just childlike trust that prompted Makar to talk: there was something of a preacher in him. I detected with glee a sly little smile he darted at the doctor or perhaps even at Versilov. This conversation was probably the continuation of a discussion they'd been having all week. Unfortunately, the fatal phrase, which had electrified me so much the day before, slipped in again and this time triggered an outbrust in me that I regret to this day.

"Perhaps even now, though," Makar went on with concentration, "I'd be frightened to meet a truly godless man, but let me tell you, Doctor, my friend, I've never really met a man like that. What I have met were restless men, for that's what they should really be called. There are all sorts of people like that and you can't tell what makes them the way they are: some are important, others are little men; some are ignorant, others are learned; and they come from all classes, even the lowest . . . but it's all restlessness. For they keep on reading all their lives, and having filled themselves with bookish wisdom, they talk and talk, although they never find answers to what's bothering them and remain in the darkness. Some of them throw themselves in so many different directions that they end by losing themselves; the hearts of others turn into stones, although there may still be dreams in them; still others become drained of thoughts and feelings but still go around sneering at everything. Some people pick out from books nothing but the little flowers, and even then only those that suit them, but they still remain restless because they could never make up their minds in the first place. And I can see that there's too much boredom in them. A poor man may be short of bread, may not have enough to keep his children alive, may sleep on rough straw, may be brutal and sinful, but still his heart may be gay and merry; while a rich man may eat and drink too much and sit on a pile of gold with nothing but gloom in his heart. A man may study all the sciences and never get rid of emptiness and gloom; indeed, I think that the more intelligence he gains, the more his gloom will thicken.

"Or let's look at it this way: people have been taught and taught ever since the creation of the world, but what have they learned in all that time to help them make the world a gayer and happier place where man can find all the joys he's longing for? What they lack, I tell you, is *beauty*. Indeed, they don't even want it. They're all lost and every one of them glories in what has brought him to his ruin. But they never think to face the only truth, although life without God is nothing but torture. What it all comes down to is that, without realizing it, they curse the only source that can brighten our life. But that won't get them anywhere because a man cannot live without worshiping something; without worshiping he cannot bear the burden of himself. And that goes for every man. So that if a man rejects God, he will have to worship an idol that may be made of wood, gold, or ideas. So those who think they don't need God are really just idol worshipers, and that's what we should call them. But there must be true atheists too; only they're much more dangerous because they come to us with the name of God on their lips. I've often heard about them, but I've never come across one yet. There are some people like that, my friends, and there should be."

As I mentioned before, the most attractive thing about him was his complete lack of affectation, his total disregard for the impression he might make: one could guess he had an almost sinless heart. There was *gaiety* in his heart and that's why there was *beauty* in him. *Gaiety* was a favorite word of his and he often used it. It's true that at times he was perhaps abnormally exalted, became filled with an unnatural fervor that might have been due, to some extent, to the fever that never really let up entirely all that time. This, however, never once diminished his inner beauty. There were also in him certain traits that seemed contradictory: side by side with his unbelievable trust, which to my great exasperation at times prevented him from detecting irony, there was a certain slyness, which showed up particularly during our arguments. For he did enjoy arguing, though not always, and then it had to be on his own peculiar terms. It was obvious that he had covered on foot large parts of Russia and had listened a great deal to what people said. But I repeat, it was religious fervor that interested him most and that's why he liked to talk about anything that might inspire it. Besides, he obviously enjoyed telling stories with that fervent religious feeling in them. I heard from him much about his own peregrinations as well as various legends about ascetics of the remote past. Although I had never heard any of these legends before, I'm sure there was much in them he'd changed or invented because for the most part he'd heard them himself from simple, illiterate folk. There were things that one simply could not accept. But, underneath his obvious additions and distortions, there was always that amazing organic unity, something expressing a deep emotion of simple people, always tremendously moving . . .

I recall, for instance, a rather lengthy story "The Life of Mary of Egypt." I'd no idea of that "Life" or, for that matter, of any such "lives" at the time. Let me say right away, I couldn't listen to that story without tears; and these weren't sentimental tears either, they were brought on by a strange ecstasy. I felt a sensation unknown and burning, perhaps like that parched sandy desert through which the saint had wandered amidst her lions. But this is not what I wanted to talk about; anyway I'm really not qualified.

Besides his tender fervor, I also liked in him certain extremely original views on various problems still controversial in our age. Once, for instance, he told me of something that had happened to a former soldier, something that he'd "almost" witnessed himself. The soldier had returned from the army to his village, only to find that he no longer liked the idea of living among peasants. Nor, for that matter, did the villagers like him. So the man became dejected, took to the bottle, and one day robbed someone somewhere. Although there was no real evidence against him, he was arrested and tried. At the trial, his lawyer had just about succeeded in having the case dismissed for lack of evidence when the accused suddenly interrupted him. "No, just a minute, wait," he said, and went on to tell everything "down to the last little grain of dust," acknowledging his guilt with tears of penitence streaming down his cheeks. The jury retired, returned, and announced: "Not guilty!" Everyone in the courtroom cried out with joy, they were so pleased with the verdict. But the former soldier just stood there as though he'd turned into a post, looking bewildered. He understood nothing of what the presiding judge told him in admonition upon releasing him. He still didn't believe it when he walked away free. He began to worry, brooded all the time, hardly ate or drank, wouldn't talk to people, and on the fifth day hanged himself. "See, that's how it feels to live with sin on your soul," Makar concluded.

I know there's nothing so special about this story and that many stories of the sort crop up in the newspapers, but what I liked about it was Makar's tone and, even more, certain of his phrases and expressions that were imbued with a new meaning. Thus, in telling of how the villagers took a dislike to the returned soldier, Makar said, "And it is well known that a soldier is a *corrupted villager.*" And later, speaking of the lawyer, who almost succeeded in having the case dismissed, he remarked: "and what's a lawyer but *a conscience for hire.*" Such phrases slipped from his lips spontaneously, without his seeming to notice them. And although they may not have expressed the feelings characteristic of the Russian people, they did indeed express Makar's own original (not borrowed) feelings. Such judgments found among the people are sometimes striking in their originality!

"And how do you look upon the sin of suicide?" I asked Makar after hearing his story about the soldier.

"Suicide is man's greatest sin," he said with a sigh, "but God alone can judge it, for only God knows what and how much a man can bear. As for us, we must pray tirelessly for that sinner. Whenever you hear of that sin, pray hard for the sinner, at least sigh for him as you turn to God, even if you never knew him — that will make your prayer all the more effective."

"But would my prayer be of any help to him since he's already condemned?"

"Who can tell? There are many — oh, so many! — people without faith who just confuse the ignorant. Don't listen to them because they themselves don't know where they're going. A prayer for a condemned man from a man still alive will reach God, and that's the truth. Just think of the plight of a man who has no one to pray for him. And so, when you pray in the evening before going to sleep, add at the end, 'Lord Jesus, have mercy on all those who have no one to pray for them.' This prayer will be heard and it will please the Lord. Also pray for all the sinners who are still alive: 'O Lord, who holdest all destinies in Thy hand, save all the unrepentant sinners.' That's also a good prayer."

I promised him I'd pray, feeling this would please him.

And indeed, he beamed with pleasure. But I hasten to note that he never spoke in a lecturing tone, never sounded like a sage talking to an immature youth. Not in the least. In fact, he was interested in what I had to say and at times listened eagerly as I held forth on all sorts of subjects; for, although I was just a "young 'un" (as he said even though he was perfectly aware that the proper word was "youth"), he always remembered that this particular "young 'un" was incomparably better educated than himself.

One thing he was very fond of talking about was "life in the wilderness," for to him living all alone in the wild was far superior to wandering around the country. I hotly disagreed, arguing that hermits were really egoists who had fled their worldly responsibilities and, instead of trying to be useful to their fellowmen, selfishly sought only their own salvation. At first he couldn't see what I meant; indeed, I suspect he didn't understand what I was talking about, and he just went on defending the advantages of being a hermit.

"Of course," he said, "at first you feel sorry for yourself in being all alone — I mean in the beginning. But with every day that goes by, you're more and more pleased you're alone, and in the end you feel you're in the presence of God."

Then I drew for him as complete a picture as I could of all the useful things a learned man, a doctor, or anyone devoting his life to the service of mankind could accomplish. I spoke with such eloquence that he became quite enthusiastic and repeatedly expressed his approval: "That's right, my boy, God bless you, it's great the way you can understand these things!" When I finished, though, he still didn't seem quite convinced. "That's all very well," he said, dragging out his words and sighing deeply, "but how many people are there who'd stick to their duties without going astray? A man may not look upon money as his god, but money can easily become a kind of half-god and is so often a mighty temptation. And then there are other temptations: women and vanity and envy. So a man may forget the great cause and try to satisfy all these little cravings. But when he's alone in the wild, it's different, for there he can harden himself and be ready for any sacrifice. Besides, my dear boy, what is there in man's world?'' he said with intense feeling. "Isn't it just a dream? It's as if men were trying to sow by spreading sand on rocky ground; only when the yellow sand sprouts will that dream of theirs come true. We have a saying like that in our part of the country. What Christ said was, 'Go and give all you have to the poor and become the servant of all men,' for if you do you'll become a thousand times richer because your happiness won't be made just of good food, rich clothes, satisfied vanity, and appeased envy; instead, it will be built on love, love multiplied by love without end. And then you will gain not just riches, not just hundreds of thousands or a million, but it will be the whole world that you will gain! Today we amass material things without ever satisfying our greed, and then we madly squander all we have amassed. But a day will come when there will be no orphans, no beggars; everyone will be like one of my own family, everyone will be my brother, and that is when I will have gained everything and everyone! Today even some of the richest and mightiest of men care nothing about how long they have been given to live because they too can no longer think up ways to spend their hours; but one day man's hours will be multiplied a thousandfold, for he will not want to lose one single moment of his life as he will live every one of them in the gaiety of his heart. And then his wisdom will come not out of books but from living in the presence of God, and our Earth will glow brighter than the sun and there will be no sadness, no sighs will be heard, and the whole world will be paradise.''

Conversations and Exhortations of Father Zossima

This passage from The Brothers Karamazov *follows immediately after the biographical notes of the Elder Zossima. (See introductory paragraph on page 168.) There is no doubt that here we have before us Dostoyevsky's religious testament.*

THE RUSSIAN MONK AND HIS POSSIBLE SIGNIFICANCE

Fathers and teachers, what is the monk? In the cultivated world the word is nowadays pronounced by some people with a jeer, and by others it is used as a term of abuse; and this contempt for the monk is growing. It is true, alas, it is true, that there are many sluggards, gluttons, profligates, and insolent beggars among monks. Educated people point to these: "You are idlers, useless members of society, you live on the labor of others, you are shameless beggars." And yet how many meek and humble monks there are, yearning for solitude and fervent prayer in peace. These are less noticed, or are passed over in silence. And how surprised men would be if I were to say that from these meek monks, who yearn for solitary prayer, the salvation of Russia will perhaps come once more. For they are in truth made ready in peace and quiet "for the day and the hour, the month and the year."

Meanwhile in their solitude they keep the image of Christ fair and undefiled, in the purity of God's truth, from the times of the Fathers of old, the Apostles, and the martyrs. And when the time comes they will show it to the tottering creeds of the world. That is a great thought. That star will rise out of the East.

That is my view of the monk, and is it false? Is it too proud? Look at the worldly and all who set themselves up above the people of God; has not God's image and His truth been distorted in them? They have science, but in science there is nothing else than the object of sense. The spiritual world, the higher part of man's being, is rejected altogether, dismissed with a sort of triumph, even with hatred. The world has proclaimed the reign of freedom, especially of late, but what do we see in this freedom of theirs? Nothing but slavery and self-destruction! For the world says, "You have desires. So satisfy them, for you have the same rights as the most rich and powerful. Don't be afraid of satisfying them, and even multiply your desires." That is the modern doctrine of the world. In that they see freedom. And what follows from this right to multiply one's desires? In the rich, isolation and spiritual suicide; in the poor, envy and murder; for they have been given rights but have not been shown the means of satisfying their wants. They maintain that the world is getting more and more united, more and more bound together in brotherly community, as it overcomes distance and sets thoughts flying through the air.

Alas, put no faith in such a bond of union. Interpreting freedom as the multiplication and rapid satisfaction of desires, men distort their own nature, for many senseless and foolish desires and habits and ridiculous fancies are fostered in them. They live only for mutual envy, for luxury and ostentation. To have dinners, visits, carriages, rank, and slaves to wait on one is looked upon as a necessity for which life, honor, and human feeling are sacrificed, and men even commit suicide if they are unable to satisfy themselves. We see the same thing among those who are not rich, but the poor drown their unsatisfied need and their envy in drunkenness. And soon they will drink blood instead of wine — they are being led on to it. I ask you — is such a man free? I knew one "champion of freedom" who told me himself that when he was deprived of tobacco in prison, he was so wretched at the privation that he almost went and betrayed his cause for the sake of getting tobacco again! And such a man says, "I am fighting for the cause of humanity."

How can such a one fight — what is he fit for? He is capable perhaps of some action quickly over, but he cannot hold out long. And it's no wonder that instead of gaining freedom they have sunk into slavery, and instead of serving the cause of brotherly love and the union of humanity, have fallen, on the contrary, into dissension and isolation, as my mysterious visitor and teacher said to me in my youth. And therefore the idea of the service of humanity, of brotherly love and the solidarity of mankind, is more and more dying out in the world, and indeed this idea is sometimes treated with derision. For how can a man shake off his habits — what can become of him if he is in such bondage to the habit of satisfying the innumerable desires he has created for himself? He is isolated, and what concern has he for the rest of humanity? They have succeeded in accumulating a greater mass of objects, but the joy in the world has grown less.

The monastic way is very different. Obedience, fasting, and prayer are laughed at, yet only through them lies the way to real, true freedom. I cut off my superfluous and unnecessary desires; I subdue my proud and wanton will and chastise it with obedience; and with God's help I attain freedom of spirit and with it spiritual joy. Who is most capable of conceiving a great idea and serving it — the rich man in his isolation or the man who has freed himself from the tyranny of material things and habits? The monk is reproached for his solitude: "You have secluded yourself within the walls of the monastery for your own salvation and have forgotten the brotherly service of humanity!" But we shall see who will be the more zealous in the cause of brotherly love. For it is not we, but they, who are in isolation, though they don't see that. Of old, leaders of the people came from among us, and why should they not again? The same meek and humble ascetics will rise up and go out to work for the great cause. The salvation of Russia comes from the people. And the Russian monk has always been on the side of the people. We are isolated only if the people are isolated. The people believe as we do, and an unbelieving reformer will never do anything in Russia, even if he is sincere in heart and a genius. Remember that! The people will meet the atheist and overcome him, and Russia will be one and orthodox. Take care of the peasant and guard his heart. Go on educating him quietly. That's your duty as monks, for the peasant has God in his heart.

OF MASTERS AND SERVANTS, AND OF WHETHER IT IS POSSIBLE FOR THEM TO BE BROTHERS IN THE SPIRIT

Of course, I don't deny that there is sin in the peasants too. And the fire of corruption is spreading visibly, hourly, working from above downward. The spirit of isolation is coming upon the people too. Moneylenders and devourers of the community are rising up. Already the merchant grows more and more eager for rank; he strives to show himself cultured though he has not a trace of culture, and to this end he meanly despises his old traditions and is even ashamed of the faith of his fathers. He visits princes, though he is only a peasant corrupted. The peasants are rotting in drunkenness and cannot shake off the habit. And what cruelty to their wives, to their children even! All from drunkenness! In the factories I've seen children of nine years old, frail, rickety, bent, and already depraved. The stuffy workshop, the din of machinery, work all day long, the vile language, and the drink, the drink — is that what a little child's heart needs? He needs sunshine, childish play, good examples all about him, and at least a little love. There must be no more of this, monks, no more torturing of children — rise up and preach that, make haste, make haste!

But God will save Russia, for though the peasants are corrupted and cannot renounce their filthy sin, yet they know it is cursed by God and that they do wrong in sinning. Have faith in God and weep tears of devotion so that our people will still believe in righteousness.

It is different with the upper classes. Following science, they want to base justice on reason alone but not, as before, with Christ, and they have already proclaimed that there is no crime, that there is no sin. And that's consistent, for if you have no God, what is the meaning of crime? In Europe the people are already rising up against the rich with violence, and the leaders of the people are everywhere leading them to bloodshed and teaching them that their wrath is righteous. But their "wrath is accursed, for it is cruel." But God will save Russia as He has saved her many times. Salvation will come from the people, from their faith and their meekness.

Fathers and teachers, watch over the people's faith, and this will not be a dream. I've been struck all my life by the dignity in our great people, their true and seemly dignity. I've seen it myself, I can testify to it. I've seen it and marveled at it; I've seen it in spite of the degraded sins and poverty-stricken appearance of our peasantry. They are not servile, and even after two centuries of serfdom they are free in manner and bearing, yet without insolence and not revengeful, not envious. "You are rich and noble, you are clever and talented — well be so, God bless you. I respect you, but I know that I too am a man. By the very fact that I respect you without envy I prove my dignity as a man."

In truth, even if they don't say this (for they don't know how to say this yet), that is how they act. I have seen it myself, I have known it myself, and would you believe it, the poorer our Russian peasant is, the more noticeable is that serene goodness, for the rich among them are for the most part corrupted already, and much of that is due to our carelessness and indifference. But God will save His people, for Russia is great in her humility. I dream of seeing our future and seem already to see it clearly. It will come to pass that even the most corrupt of our rich will end by being ashamed of his riches before the poor, and the poor, seeing his humility, will understand and give way before him, will respond joyfully and kindly to his honorable shame. Believe me that it will end in that; things are moving to that. Equality is to be found only in the spiritual dignity of man, and that will be understood only among us. If we were brothers, there would be fraternity, but until then they will never agree about the division of wealth. We preserve the image of Christ, and it will shine forth like a precious diamond to the whole world. So may it be, so may it be!

Fathers and teachers, a touching incident befell me once. In my wanderings I met in the town of K. my old orderly, Afanasy. It was eight years since I had parted from him. He chanced to see me in the marketplace, recognized me, ran up to me, and how delighted he was; he simply pounced on me: "Master dear, is it you? Is it really you I see?" He took me home with him.

He was no longer in the army; he was married and already had two little children. He and his wife earned their living as vendors in the marketplace. His room was poor, but bright and clean. He made me sit down, set the samovar, and sent for his wife as though my appearance were a festival for them. He brought me his children: "Bless them, Father."

"Is it for me to bless them; I am only a humble monk. I will pray for them. And for you, Afanasy Pavlovitch, I have prayed every day since that day, for it all came from you," said I. And I explained that to him as well as I could. And what do you think? The man kept gazing at me and could not believe that I, his former master, an officer, was now before him in such a guise and position; it made him shed tears.

"Why are you weeping?" said I, "better rejoice over me, dear friend, whom I can never forget, for my path is a glad and joyful one."

He did not say much but kept sighing and shaking his head over me tenderly.

"What has become of your fortune?" he asked.

"I gave it to the monastery," I answered; "we live in common."

After tea I began saying good-bye. Suddenly he brought out half a ruble as an offering to the monastery, and I saw him hurriedly thrusting another half-ruble into my hand: "That's for you in your wanderings; it may be of use to you, Father."

I took his half-ruble, bowed to him and his wife, and went out rejoicing. And on my way I thought: "Here we both are now, he at home and I on the road, sighing and shaking our heads, no doubt, and yet smiling joyfully in the gladness of our hearts, remembering how God brought about our meeting."

I have never seen him since. I had been his master and he my servant, but now when we exchanged a loving kiss with softened hearts, there was a great human bond between us. I have thought a great deal about that, and what I think now is this: is it so inconceivable that that grand and simplehearted unity might in due time become universal among the Russian people? I believe that it will come to pass and that the time is at hand.

And of servants I will add this: in old days when I was young I was often angry with servants — "the cook had served something too hot, the orderly had not brushed my clothes." But what then taught me better was a thought of my dear brother's that I had heard from him in childhood: "Am I worth it that another should serve me and be ordered about by me in his poverty and ignorance?" And I wondered at the time that such simple and self-evident ideas should be so slow to occur to our minds.

It is impossible that there should be no servants in the world; but act so that your servant may be freer in spirit than if he were not a servant. And why cannot I be a servant to my servant and even let him see it, and that without any pride on my part or any mistrust on his? Why should not my servant be like my own kindred, so that I may take him into my family and rejoice in doing so? Even now this can be done, but it will lead to the grand unity of men in the future, when a man will not seek servants for himself or desire to turn his fellow creatures into servants as he does now but, on the contrary will long with his whole heart to be the servant of all, as the Gospel teaches.

And can it be a dream that in the end man will find his joy only in deeds of light and mercy and not in cruel pleasures as now — in gluttony, fornication, ostentation, boasting, and envious rivalry of one with the other? I firmly believe that it is not a dream and that the time is at hand. People laugh and ask, "When will that time come and does it look like coming?" I believe that with Christ's help we shall accomplish this great thing. And how many ideas there have been on earth in the history of man that were unthinkable ten years before they appeared? Yet when their destined hour had come, they came forth and spread over the whole earth. So it will be with us, and our people will shine forth in the world, and all men will say, "The stone which the builders rejected has become the cornerstone of the building."

And we may ask the scornful themselves: if our hope is a dream, when will you build up your edifice and order things justly by your intellect alone, without Christ? If they declare that it is they who are advancing toward unity, only the most simplehearted among them believe it, so that one may positively marvel at such simplicity. Of a truth, they have more fantastic dreams than we. They aim at justice, but denying Christ, they will end by flooding the earth with blood, for blood cries out for blood, and he that taketh up the sword shall perish by the sword. And if it were not for Christ's covenant, they would slaughter one another down to the last two men on earth. And those two last men would not be able to restrain each other in their pride, and the one would slay the other and then himself. And that would come to pass were it not for the promise of Christ that for the sake of the humble and meek the days shall be shortened.

While I was still wearing an officer's uniform after my duel, I talked about servants in general society, and I remember everyone was amazed at me. "What!" they asked, "Are we to make our servants sit down on the sofa and offer them tea?" And I answered them: "Why not, sometimes at least." Everyone laughed. Their question was frivolous and my answer was not clear, but the thought in it was to some extent right.

OF PRAYER, OF LOVE, AND OF CONTACT WITH OTHER WORLDS

Young man, be not forgetful of prayer. Every time you pray, if your prayer is sincere, there will be new feeling and new meaning in it that will give you fresh courage, and you will understand that prayer is an education. Remember too, every day and whenever you can, to repeat to yourself, "Lord, have mercy on all who appear before Thee today." For every hour and every moment thousands of men leave life on this earth, and their souls appear before God. And how many of them depart in solitude, unknown, sad, and dejected, so no one mourns for them or even knows whether they have lived or not. And behold, from the other end of the earth perhaps, your prayer for their rest will rise up to God, though you knew them not nor they you. How touching it must be to a soul standing in dread before the Lord to feel at that instant that for him too there is one to pray, that there is a fellow creature left on earth to love him. And God will look on you both more graciously, for if you have had so much pity on him, how much more will He have pity Who is infinitely more loving and merciful than you. And He will forgive him for your sake.

Brothers, have no fear of men's sin. Love a man even in his sin, for that is the semblance of Divine Love and is the highest love on earth. Love all God's creation, the whole and every grain of sand in it. Love every leaf, every ray of God's light. Love the animals, love the plants, love everything. If you love everything, you will perceive the divine mystery in things. Once you perceive it, you will begin to comprehend it better every day. And you will come at last to love the whole world with an all-embracing love. Love the animals — God has given them the rudiments of thought and joy untroubled.

Do not trouble them — don't harass them, don't deprive them of their happiness, don't work against God's intent. Man, do not pride yourself on superiority to the animals; they are without sin, while you with your greatness defile the earth by your appearance on it and leave the traces of your foulness after you — alas, it is true of almost every one of us! Love children especially, for they too are sinless like the angels; they live to soften and purify our hearts and, as it were, to guide us. Woe to him who offends a child! Father Anfim taught me to love children. The kind, silent man used often on our wanderings to spend the farthings given us on sweets and cakes for the children. He could not pass by a child without emotion; that's the nature of the man.

At some thoughts one stands perplexed, especially at the sight of men's sin, and asks oneself whether one should use force or love and humility. Always decide to use humble love. If you resolve on that once and for all, you may subdue the whole world. Loving humility is marvelously strong, the strongest of all things, and there is nothing else like it.

Every day and every hour, every minute, walk round yourself and watch yourself, and see that your image is a seemly one. You pass by a little child, you pass by with ugly and spiteful words, with wrathful heart; you may not have noticed the child, but he has seen you, and your image, revolting and godless, may remain in his defenseless heart. You don't know it, but you may have sown an evil seed in him and it may grow, all because you were not careful before the child, because you did not foster in yourself a careful, actively benevolent love. Brothers, love is a teacher; but one must know how to acquire it, for it is hard to acquire, it is dearly bought, it is won slowly by long labor. For we must love not only occasionally, for a moment, but forever. Everyone can love occasionally, even the wicked can.

My brother asked the birds to forgive him: that sounds

senseless, but it is right; for all is like an ocean, all is flowing and blending; a touch in one place sets up movement at the other end of the earth. It may be senseless to beg forgiveness of the birds, but birds would be happier at your side — a little happier, anyway — and children and all animals, if you yourself were nobler than you are now. It's all like an ocean, I tell you. Then you would pray to the birds too, consumed by an all-embracing love in a sort of transport, and pray that they too will forgive you your sin. Treasure this ecstasy, however senseless it may seem to men.

My friends, pray to God for gladness. Be glad as children, as the birds of heaven. And let not the sin of men disturb you in your actions. Fear not that it will wear away your work and hinder you from accomplishing it. Do not say, "Sin is mighty, wickedness is mighty, evil environment is mighty; we are lonely and helpless, and evil environment is wearing us away and hindering our good work from being done." Fly from that dejection, children! There is only one means of salvation: take yourself and make yourself responsible for all men's sins — friends, that is the truth, you know, for as soon as you sincerely make yourself responsible for everything and for all men, you will see at once that it is really so and that you are to blame for everyone and for all things. But by throwing your own indolence and impotence on others you will end up sharing the pride of Satan and murmuring against God.

Of the pride of Satan I think this: it is hard for us on earth to comprehend it, and therefore it is so easy to fall into error and to share it, even imagining that we are doing something grand and fine. Indeed on earth, we cannot comprehend many of the strongest feelings and movements of our nature. Let not that be a stumbling block, and think not that it may serve as a justification to you for anything. For the Eternal Judge asks of you what you can comprehend and not what you cannot. You will know that yourself hereafter, for you will behold all things truly then and will not dispute them. On earth, however, we are as it were astray, and if it were not for the precious image of Christ before us, we should be undone and altogether lost, like the human race before the flood. Much on earth is hidden from us, but to make up for that we have been given a mysterious hidden longing for our living bond with the other world, with the higher heavenly world, and the roots of our thoughts and feelings are not here but in other worlds. That is why the philosophers say that we cannot apprehend the reality of things on earth.

God took seeds from different worlds and sowed them on this earth, and His garden grew, and everything came up that could come up, but all growing things live and are alive only through the feeling of their contact with other mysterious worlds. If that feeling grows weak or is destroyed in you, what has grown up in you will die. Then you will become indifferent to life and even grow to hate it. That's what I think.

CAN A MAN JUDGE HIS FELLOW CREATURES? FAITH TO THE END

Remember particularly that you cannot be a judge of anyone. For no one can judge a criminal until he recognizes that he is just such a criminal as the man standing before him and that he, perhaps more than all men, is to blame for that crime. When he understands that, he will be able to be a judge. Though that sounds absurd, it is true. If I had been righteous myself, perhaps there would have been no criminal standing before me. If you can take upon yourself the crime of the criminal whom your heart is judging, take it at once, suffer for him yourself, and let him go without reproach. And even if the law itself makes you his judge, act in the same spirit so far as possible, for he will go away and condemn himself more bitterly than you have done. If after you kiss he goes away untouched, mocking at you, do not let that be a stumbling block to you. It shows his time has not yet come, but it will come in due course. And if it doesn't come, no matter: if not he, then another in his place will understand and suffer, and judge and condemn himself; then justice will be fulfilled. Believe that, believe it without doubt; for in that lies all the hope and faith of the saints.

Work without ceasing. If you remember in the night as you go to sleep, "I have not done what I ought to have done," rise up at once and do it. If the people around you are spiteful and callous and will not hear you, fall down before them and beg their forgiveness; for in truth you are to blame for their not wanting to hear you. And if you cannot speak to them in their bitterness, serve them in silence and in humility, never losing hope. If all men abandon you and even drive you away by force, then when you are left alone, fall on the earth and kiss it; water it with your tears, and it will bring forth fruit even though no one has seen or heard you in your solitude. Believe to the end, even if all men went astray and you were left the only one faithful; bring your offering even then and praise God in your loneliness. And if two of you are gathered together — then there is a whole world, a world of living love. Embrace each other tenderly and praise God, for if only in you two, His truth has been fulfilled.

If you sin yourself and grieve even unto death for your sins or for your sudden sin, then rejoice for others, rejoice for the righteous man, rejoice that even if you have sinned, he is righteous and has not sinned.

If the evildoing of men moves you to indignation and overwhelming distress, even to a desire for vengeance on the evildoers, shun that feeling above all things. Go at once and seek suffering for yourself, as though you were yourself guilty of that wrong. Accept that suffering and bear it, and your heart will find comfort, and you will understand that you too are guilty, for you might have been a light to the evildoers, even as the one sinless man, and you were not a light to them. If you had been a light, you would have lightened the path for others too, and the evildoer might perhaps have been saved by your light from his sin. And even though your light was shining, yet you see men were not saved by it; hold firm and doubt not the power of the heavenly light. Believe that if they were not saved, they will be saved hereafter. And if they are not saved hereafter, then their sons will be saved, for your light will not die even when you are dead. The righteous man departs, but his light remains. Men find deliverance even after the death of their deliverer. Men reject their prophets and slay them, but they love their martyrs and honor those whom they have slain. You are working for the whole, you are acting for the future. Seek no reward, for your reward on this earth is already great: the spiritual joy which is only vouchsafed to the righteous man. Fear not the great nor the mighty, but be wise and ever serene. Know the measure, know the times, study them. When you are left alone, pray. Love to throw yourself on the earth and kiss it. Kiss the earth and love it with an unceasing, consuming love. Love all men, love everything. Seek that rapture and ecstasy. Water the earth with the tears of your joy, and love those tears. Don't be ashamed of that ecstasy; prize it, for it is a gift of God and a great one; it is not given to many but only to the elect.

OF HELL AND HELLFIRE, A MYSTIC REFLECTION

Fathers and teachers, I ponder, "What is hell?" I maintain that it is the suffering of being unable to love. Once in infinite existence, immeasurable in time and space, a spiritual creature on his coming to earth, was given the power of saying, "I am and I love." Once, only once, there was given him a moment of active *living* love, and for that earthly life was given him and with it times and seasons. And that happy creature rejected the priceless gift, prized and loved it not, scorned it and remained callous. Such a one, having left the earth, sees Abraham's bosom and talks with Abraham, as we are told in the parable of the rich man and Lazarus, and beholds heaven and can go up to the Lord. But that is just his torment, to rise up to the Lord without ever having loved, to be brought close to those who have loved when he has despised their love. For he sees clearly and says to himself, "Now I have understanding, and though I now thirst to love, there will be nothing great, no sacrifice in my love, for my earthly life is over, and Abraham will not come even with a drop of living water (that is the gift of earthly, active life) to cool the fiery thirst of spiritual love which burns in me now, though I despised it on earth; there is no more life for me and there will be no more time! Even though I would gladly give my life for others, it can never be, for that life which can be sacrificed for love is past, and now there is a gulf fixed between that life and this existence."

They talk of hellfire in the material sense. I don't go into that mystery, and I shun it. But I think if there were fire in a material sense, they would be glad of it, for I imagine, that in material agony their still greater spiritual agony would be forgotten for a moment. Moreover, that spiritual agony cannot be taken from them, for that suffering is not external but within them. And if it could be taken from them, I think it would be bitterer still for the unhappy creatures. For even if the righteous in Paradise forgave them, beholding their torments, and called them up to heaven in their infinite love, they would only multiply their torments, for they would arouse in them still more keenly a flaming thirst for responsive, active, and grateful love, which is now impossible. In the timidity of my heart I imagine, however, that the very recognition of this impossibility would at last serve to console them. For by accepting the love of the righteous with no possibility of repaying it — by this submissiveness and the effect of this humility — they will at last attain to a certain semblance of that active love which they scorned in life, to something like its outward expression . . . I am sorry, friends and brothers, that I cannot express this clearly. But woe to those who have slain themselves on earth, woe to the suicides! I believe that there can be none more miserable than they. They tell us that it is a sin to pray for them, and outwardly the Church, as it were, renounces them, but in my secret heart I believe that we may pray even for them. Love can never be an offense to Christ. I have prayed inwardly all my life for such as those; I confess it, fathers and teachers, and even now I pray for them every day.

Oh, there are some who remain proud and fierce even in hell, in spite of their certain knowledge and contemplation of the absolute truth; there are some fearful ones who have given themselves over to Satan and his proud spirit entirely. For such, hell is voluntary and ever-consuming; they are tortured by their own choice. For they have cursed themselves, cursing God and life. They live upon their vindictive pride like a starving man in the desert sucking blood out of his own body. But they are never satisfied, and they refuse forgiveness; they curse God Who calls them. They cannot behold the living God without hatred, and they cry out that the God of life should be annihilated, that God should destroy Himself and His own creation. And they will burn in the fire of their own wrath forever and yearn for death and annihilation. But they will not attain to death . . .

Afterword

Extracts From the German Edition
By Karl Nötzel, Editor

Like Tolstoy, Dostoyevsky had been a religious church member when a child, but already as a young man he had turned to the progressive beliefs of Russian intellectuals of the time. Later he gained a very deep insight into the horrors of human misery and called God himself into question, the God who allowed it all. Dostoyevsky, champion of the innocent sufferer, still lacked the selflessness needed to accept God without rebellion. Spiritual pride seems to have held him back, plus injured self-esteem.

All this lost its importance for him before the firing squad and most of all during the near decade in Siberia, first in prison and then in exile.

In his last great masterpieces Dostoyevsky shows the wounded soul the way to healing, which is to be unavenging. Such a person is thereby immediately immune to attack — to the helpless amazement of all, and is most clearly portrayed in the character of Prince Myshkin in *The Idiot*.

So he passes beyond revenge. By doing so he is now able to see all of the reality that is not God, in a relationship to God that will never be lost.

In Dostoyevsky, the search for the meaning of life turns into the question of faith in God — not of God's existence. For knowledge of God is simply inescapable. And faith in

God really means only acknowledging Him. For if God is God, the spiritual origin of all that is, there is an absolute chasm between God and man. This is the meaning of "The Legend of the Grand Inquisitor," which without question is Dostoyevsky's statement of his deepest religious faith.

The true content and context of Dostoyevsky's great works is man's struggle to find God, in the face of every imaginable temptation to deny Him. But man is shown the way to God through the man Christ alone. Through Christ God speaks to us.

Fyodor Dostoyevsky
Biographical Sketch

November 11, 1821, born in Moscow, son of a staff doctor at a charity hospital.

1838, entered army engineering college in St. Petersburg (Leningrad). Did not like this training, read much literature.

June 1839, his father was murdered by his own serfs, who had been brutally mistreated.

October 1844, gave up army commission to finish first novel, *Poor Folk*, in April 1845. Praise by the critic Belinski brought immediate success.

1849, his participation in a revolutionary group was punished by four years in a Siberian prison.

1850s, epilepsy developed.

1854 to 1858, stayed on in Siberia. Wrote "Uncle's Dream" and "Friend of the Family" while there.

February 6, 1857, first marriage a failure.

1859, returned to St. Petersburg. Published a monthly periodical called *Time*.

1866, *Crime and Punishment* put Dostoyevsky in the front rank of Russian writers.

February 15, 1867, three years after his first wife's death, Dostoyevsky married a young stenographer, who proved to be a good manager of his finances. Of their four children, two died very early.

1868-69, almost unnoticed by Russian critics, Dostoyevsky's

novel *The Idiot* is one of his most discerning and power-ful. Published in a period of revolutionary agitation, its universal theme — a good man in human society — was not considered timely.

1874–75, the reception of *The Adolescent* (or *A Raw Youth*) was unfriendly.

1879–80, his genius was immediately seen in his last and greatest novel *The Brothers Karamazov.*

1870's, in Dostoyevsky's last years, revolutionary activity in Russia was increasing, with attempts on the life of the Czar and high state officials. He became very conservative, edited a conservative weekly, and felt that Russia and the Orthodox Church alone were fated to lead Europe and the world from evil to the good.

February 9, 1881, died in St. Petersburg.

About the Bruderhof

Basis   Despite all that troubles our society, we must witness to the fact that God's spirit is at work in the world today. God still calls men and women away from the systems of injustice to his justice, and away from the old ways of violence, fear, and isolation to a new way of peace, love, and brotherhood. In short, he calls us to community.

The basis of our communal life is Christ's Sermon on the Mount and his other New Testament teachings, in particular those concerning brotherly love and love of enemies, mutual service, nonviolence and the refusal to bear arms, sexual purity, and faithfulness in marriage. Instead of holding assets or property privately, we share everything in common, the way the early Christians did as recorded in the Book of Acts. Each member gives his or her talents, time, and efforts wherever they are needed. Money and possessions are pooled voluntarily, and in turn each member is provided for and cared for. Lunch and dinner are eaten together, and meetings for fellowship, singing, prayer, or decision making are held several evenings a week.

Family Life   Although many of our members are single adults, the family is the primary unit of our community. Children are a central part of our life together. Parents are primarily responsible for educating them, but teachers, as all adult members of our communities, support them with encouragement and, where necessary, guidance. In this way, problems can be solved, burdens carried, and joys shared.

During work hours, babies and small children receive daily care in our "Children's House"; elementary and middle school grades (K–8) are educated in our own schools. Teens attend public high school and then move on to university, college, or technical/vocational training. Some young adults find work in mission service projects and return with valuable knowledge and experience.

Our disabled, invalid, and elderly members are a treasured part of the community. Whether participating in the communal work (even if only for a few hours a day) or remaining at home, where they are often visited by children, they enrich our life in a vital way.

Work   Our life is a joyful one, as full of the sounds of song and play as of work. We earn our living by manufacturing and selling Community Playthings (a line of play equipment and furniture for children) and Rifton Equipment for People with Disabilities. Other enterprises include a charter flight service and breeding kennels. To us, our work is far more than a business venture, however. From washing clothes and dishes to assembling products in our workshops or caring for children, it is a practical expression of our love for one another.

Roots   The roots of the Bruderhof go back to the time of the Radical Reformation of early 16th-century Europe, when thousands of so-called Anabaptists left the institutional church to seek a life of simplicity, brotherhood, and nonviolence. One branch of this dissident movement, known as Hutterites after their leader Jakob Hutter, settled in communal villages or Bruderhofs ("place of brothers") in Moravia. Here their excellent craftsmanship, their advanced medical skills, their agricultural successes, and their progressive schools brought them widespread renown.

Recent History   In 1920, Eberhard Arnold, a well-known lecturer and writer, left the security of his Berlin career and moved with his wife and children to Sannerz, a tiny German village, to found a small community based on the practices of the early church. Though the Arnolds were not directly influenced by the early Hutterites in founding their new settlement, they soon discovered that Hutterian Bruderhofs still existed (now in North America), and they initiated a relationship that lasts to this day.

Despite persecution by the Nazis and the turmoil of World War II, the community survived. Amid increasing difficulties in Germany (and expulsion in 1937), new Bruderhofs were founded in England in the late 1930s. With the outbreak of World War II a second migration was necessary, this time to Paraguay, the only country willing to accept our multinational group. During the 1950s branch communities were started in the United States and Europe. In 1960-61 the South American communities were closed, and members relocated to Europe and the United States.

The Present Today there are three Bruderhofs in New York, one in Connecticut, two in Pennsylvania, and two in southeastern England. We are insignificant in numbers, yet we believe our task is of utmost importance: to follow Jesus and, in a society that has turned against him, to build up a new society guided by his spirit of love. Our movement struggles forward against the stream of contemporary society — and against the obstacles our human weaknesses continually place in the way — yet God has held us together through times of external persecution, internal struggle, and spiritual decline, and we entrust our future to him.

Outreach At a local level, we are involved in voluntary community service projects and prison ministry. On a broader scale, our contacts with other fellowships and community groups have taken us to many places around the globe, especially in recent years. Mission has always been a vital focus of our activity, though not in the sense of trying to convert people or to recruit new members. The connections we make with others outside our communities — with all men and women who strive for brotherhood, no matter what their creed — are just as important to us. Naturally, we welcome every person who is seeking something new in his or her life. Come join us for a weekend.

Vision Though we come from many cultures, countries, and walks of life, we are all brothers and sisters. We are conscious of our shortcomings as individuals and as a community, yet we believe that it is possible to live out in deeds Jesus' clear way of love, freedom, and truth not only on Sundays, but from day to day. With Eberhard Arnold we affirm:

> This planet, the earth, must be conquered for a new kingdom, a new social order, a new unity, a new joy. Joy comes to us from God, who is the God of love, who is the spirit of peace, unity, and community. This is the message

Jesus brings. And we must have the faith and the certainty that his message is valid still today.

The Plough Publishing House Our publishing house, which is owned and run by Bruderhof members, sells books about radical Christian discipleship, community, marriage, child rearing, social justice, and the spiritual life. We also publish a small periodical, *The Plough*, with articles on current issues the mainstream media tends to ignore, and reflective pieces on personal and societal transformation. Sample copies or a subscription are available free on request, though we welcome donations to meet costs.

Information For more information, or to arrange a visit, write or call us at either of the following addresses. We can give you the address and telephone number of the Bruderhof nearest you:

The Plough Publishing House
Spring Valley Bruderhof
Route 381 North
Farmington PA 15437-9506 USA

Toll free: 1-800-521-8011
Tel: 412-329-1100

The Plough Publishing House
Darvell Bruderhof
Robertsbridge, E. Sussex
TN32 5DR United Kingdom

Toll free: 0800-269-048
Tel: +44(0)1580-881-003

URL: www.bruderhof.org

Other Titles from Plough

A Plea for Purity: Sex, Marriage, and God by Johann Christoph Arnold. Thoughts on relationships, sex, marriage, divorce, abortion, homosexuality, and other related issues from a biblical perspective.

A Little Child Shall Lead Them by Johann Christoph Arnold. A welcome approach to child rearing based on the biblical idea of "becoming a child" and, building on that, bringing up children with reverence for their child-likeness.

I Tell You A Mystery by Johann Christoph Arnold. Drawing on stories of people he has known and counseled as pastor, relative, or friend, Arnold shows how suffering can be given meaning, and despair overcome. He offers the assurance that even today, in our culture of isolation and death, there is such a thing as hope.

God's Revolution by Eberhard Arnold. Topically arranged excerpts from the author's talks and writings on the church, community, marriage and family issues, government, and world suffering.

Salt and Light by Eberhard Arnold. Talks and writings on the transformative power of a life lived by Jesus' revolutionary teachings in the Sermon on the Mount.

Discipleship by J. Heinrich Arnold. A collection of thoughts on following Christ in the daily grind, topically arranged. Includes sections on love, humility, forgiveness, leadership, gifts, community, sexuality, marriage, parenting, illness, suffering, mission, salvation, and the kingdom of God.

The Early Christians by Eberhard Arnold. Letters and sayings of the early church in the words of its own members. Includes material from a variety of contemporary sources.

The Meaning and Power of Prayer Life by Eberhard Arnold. Thoughts on prayer not as a "pious exercise," but as a springboard for day-to-day living.

Freedom from Sinful Thoughts by J. Heinrich Arnold. Biblically-based advice for men and women who desire help in overcoming unwanted fantasies and temptations.

The Individual and World Need by Eberhard Arnold. A revolutionary essay that explores the relationship of the individual to suffering and sin on a global scale.

Why We Live in Community by Eberhard Arnold, with two interpretive talks by Thomas Merton. Inspirational thoughts on the basis, meaning, and purpose of community.

Love and Marriage in the Spirit by Eberhard Arnold. Talks and essays on the importance of faith as a basis for meaningful and lasting Christian relationships.

Inner Land by Eberhard Arnold. Timeless essays on the "inner land of the invisible" where men and women may find strength and courage to follow God's call in today's world.

To order, or to request a complete catalog, call:

United States
Toll free: 1-800-521-8011
Tel: 412-329-1100

United Kingdom
Free phone: 0800-269-048
Tel: +44(0)1580-881-003

URL: www.bruderhof.org